Uprooting Fear

The Heart's Accidental Journey to the Divine

AURA CAMACHO-MAAS

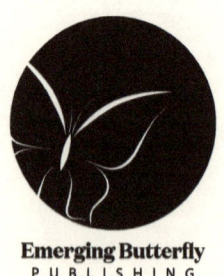

Contents

ONE: The Face of Fear 1

TWO: Into the Light 41

THREE: An Oracle Appears 55

FOUR: The World of Doing 69

FIVE: Revelations 103

SIX: The Dark Night of the Senses 123

SEVEN: Shamanism 149

EIGHT: The Dark Night of Spirit 167

NINE: The World of Being 179

TEN: Divinity 197

ELEVEN: Transcendence 223

Copyright ©2020 Aura Camacho-Maas
All rights reserved. No part of this book may be reproduced or utilized in any form or by any means, electronic, or mechanical, without permission in writing from the author except in the case of brief quotations used in critical articles or reviews.

Author contact: www.auracamachomaas.com

ISBN 978-1-7346226-0-7
First Edition: 2020 v3.19

10 9 8 7 6 5 4 3 2 1

Colophon
Body text composed in Adobe Minion Pro (variable concept) 12/18. Titles, subtitles, and captions in Adobe Futura Book.

All images by the author.

Dedication

To Spirit. To my husband.

"We all are searching to become better human beings. Many in the constant search find the tools that light the path. Others simply continue in darkness because they don't know how and where to search. From the beginning, this shocking story grabs and immerses the reader in the internal discoveries of the author that are both personal and universal. This story can help many people."

—Janeth Charris, Colombia

"I read it twice. And I will keep on reading it again and again. So easy to read and very interesting indeed."

—Rose Carr, England

"I loved reading your book! Overall, there are many great life lessons and deep thoughts to consider which I thoroughly enjoyed."

—Shirley Okereke, USA

"I admire the author for her tenacity and perseverance to write this perfect narrative that keeps the reader in suspense from the beginning to the end. This book is a spiritual work of art!"

—Aura Stella Tumbridge, USA

"I love it. The writing is so strong, authentic and honest."

—Mary Ryan, Ireland

"An engrossing, deeply personal and immensely universal story."

—Jamie Eggleston, USA

Acknowledgments

My heart is full of gratitude toward all who have crossed my path. Through my interactions with them, I've come to know and understand that All is One and Divine.

I am grateful to my parents Luis and Cecilia, for carrying me into the World and teaching me about the power of choice.

To my brothers for sharing a common space as we grew up together in the universe of my immediate family, and to my youngest brother Juan Carlos for teaching me about compassion and about letting go.

To my dear friends Ruth and Norman Don and Richard (Dick) and Gina Wilson for their openness and for giving me of their sacred space for my evolution.

To Juan Agustin Fernandez, Enrique Flores Sinuiri, Pasquel Florez Agustin, Jose Stevens, Modesto y Toribio Quispe Lunasco, Miguel Ruiz, Ken Wilber, and Manuela Fernandez Maynas "Yanacita" for encountering them on my spiritual path.

To Doctors Alan N. Carlson and Glenn Jaffe for taking care of my sight and giving me my 20/20 vision of the World.

To Senator William (Bill) Martin and William C. Friday for their inspiration and support.

To Chuck Davis with his African American Dance Ensemble for his loving and enthusiastic support and guidance and Lloyd (Madafo) Wilson for his storytelling.

To Arnold Richardson, Ruth Revels, and the Guilford Native American Dance Group for sharing their Native American perspective and culture.

To the members of the Ballet Folklórico de Colombia and its directors Ligia de Granados and Nicoyembe for bringing their musical and cultural visions to the people of North Carolina.

To Michael S. Ward, the former North Carolina Superintendent of Education for his understanding and support of my education initiatives.

To James (Jim) F. Goodmon, the CEO of Capitol Broadcasting, Loretta Harper-Arnold, and David Crabtree for their support and outreach to the Latin American community, and Mark Schultz of the *Herald-Sun* for his collaboration on *My Identity*.

To Dorothy Albright, Lisa Bluedeer, Oscar Borrero-Ochoa, Nila Chamberlain, Tom Cook, Maria Earnshaw, Lilia Espinosa-Tyson, Ricardo Gaitan Orjuela, Ricardo Granillo,

Gladys Graves, William Hill, Vivia Lawson, Margarita Jimenez, Larry Mabe, Betty Mangum, Adriana Montbrun, Mary Lee Moore, Jim O'Reilly, Kathleen O'Toole, Mary Ryan, Mark Spano, Dan Strickland, Purnell Swett, David Tyson, Tim Turner, Rick Walsh, Sheila Wright, and Gabriela Zabala for believing and supporting me in my work.

To Renato Basile, Rose Carr, Sande Johnson, David Krieger, and Salvador Ros Garcia for their patience and encouragement in reading my early writings.

To Peggy Payne for her developmental editing and encouraging me to connect the mystical aspects of my story, Susan Remek for challenging me to have the courage to call myself a mystic, Georgann Eubanks and Judy Dearlove for connecting me to the world of publishing, and Shirley Okereke for offering great marketing insights, advice, and editorial comments.

To Alan Scott for his invaluable insights and the exquisite touch he brought to the book's design and publishing process.

To my husband John for his tireless reading and editing of my writing and for his divine grace, integrity, and unconditional support. For being the personification of LOVE.

> Promise:
> If I read you
> what I wrote bear
> in mind I wrote it
> down only
> so that
> I remember.
>
> —Oglala Lakota,
> from *Whereas by Layli Long Soldier*

> "Nothing in life is to be feared—it is only to be understood. Now is the time to understand more, so that we may fear less."
>
> —Attributed to Maria Skłodowska-Curie

Prologue

We live in a culture of fear. If unresolved, fear, with the force of an ancient glacier, will continue to carve the landscape of our life experiences. We must release the fear that for eons has accumulated in our heart.

This is a true story about what happened to me as I learned to acknowledge and honor fear and find love, guided by Spirit as the life-giving creative force permeating all that is and is to become. I learned that love and fear are the emotional forces at each end of the human experience.

I was born in Bogotá, Colombia in what felt like a boiling cauldron of fear and emotional pain caused by my father's rage and my mother's emotional distance. Growing up, whenever I felt sad, angry, or even happy, my father would sense my mood and immediately and condemningly say to me "Que le pasa?" "What's the matter with you?" When I turned to my mom with open heart for help, she always walked away.

Growing up in this environment, guidance from my soul started from almost inaudible whispers, growing louder and louder, expanding my emerging consciousness. I, in tiny steps, became able to extract fear out of conflict, and I gradually found what I needed for my soul's evolution.

You will read about these early experiences as a child and young adult in the first few chapters as a deeply personal yet broadly universal story. It provides a foundation of understanding for all that comes later about fear, education, and spiritual growth.

In later chapters you will read that the basis for all that I must tell lies with four revelations and the access to ancestral wisdom around them that have made my life a mystical experience.

Take my words to heart. They show a way out of our abyss of fear and the path to the Divine.

ONE

The Face of Fear

Colombia, South America

As a child, I looked forward to Saturdays when my parents, early in the morning, went to the market and came back with bags of fresh fruits and vegetables. Their aroma invaded and freshened the air in our house. My three older brothers and I were already going to neighborhood schools and were quite involved in all sorts of extracurricular activities. I danced a lot. Life felt good.

Matilde was our nanny, and she took care of us while my parents worked shifts at the textile factory where they met. She lived with us for six years until my mother left her job and became a homemaker. I loved Matilde dearly. She must have been an angel delivered by Spirit to cast a positive influence on my life. Sadly, I lost contact with her and her stories of my life as a child.

One afternoon when I was around seven or eight years old, I came home from school, and following my regular routine, looked for my parents to say hello. After checking in different rooms in our rather large house, I heard a loud radio playing somewhere. Following the sound, I found myself in front of my parents' bedroom. The door was closed, and my curiosity got the best of me. I carefully opened the door a crack to look inside. I never could have been prepared for what came next.

Aghast, I saw my mother lying on the floor sobbing, and my father kneeling over her pointing at her head with a gun. I stormed in, and without hesitation, threw my body between them. I met my father's wide opened eyes in disbelief. I began screaming, begging him "No dispare papi, por favor no dispare!" "Don't pull the trigger papa, please don't shoot."

My sudden appearance and reaction stopped my father in his tracks. Almost like a child who is discovered acting mischievously, he got up and sheepishly put his gun aside. My mother and I also stood up. No one said a word, and everyone left the room and went in different directions in the house. A bit later someone slammed a door, and I knew my father had left the house. My heart was brutally awakened! That night my mother quietly came into my bedroom and went to sleep with me, something that foretold my role of becoming the parent to my parents.

I gathered that the reason for the fight was that, through her friends from her old job, my mother heard of my father's relationship with another woman, and that he was planning to marry her. I saw my mom's world turned upside down as she realized that my father, whom she adored, was a womanizer and a drinker. From that moment on, I saw that my mother was torn between yielding to my father's mighty control, maintaining her relationship with him, and acting on her children's behalf.

Dreadful fights and loving reconciliations became familiar. After a big fight, my father went out drinking, hired some street musicians and showed up with them in the middle of the night under the balcony outside of their bedroom. A serenade broke the silence with a set of romantic, very romantic, songs. I would peek through the blinds to see my father's happy if drunken face and that of the musicians. I loved the music, and he sometimes joined in the singing. The song's lyrics conveyed my father's love for my mother. My father was saying "I am sorry. Please forgive me." She always did, and they would sit on a couch in the living room telling each other "I love you."

I actually enjoyed these occasions. They seemed happy and full of anticipation of permanent reconciliation. And I felt peace in their truce. I enjoyed my parent's reconciliation rituals. There seemed to be love between them. I deluded myself that their relationship was healed until they always began fighting again.

Moments of family enjoyment and camaraderie were rare, short lived and they mostly involved something to do with music and dancing.

My earliest memories are of a grand celebration of my baptism, and later my brothers' and my First Communions. On those occasions my parents, the guests, and we children all danced throughout the night to the beat of live music performed by a band of blind musicians. What a spectacle!

There was little religiosity about these occasions since my father considered himself an atheist and my mother, I believe, bowing to my father's credo, a restrained Catholic.

There were times when we could be laughing our heads off like when our nanny found out that my youngest and fun-loving and entertaining brother had adopted an abandoned horse he found somewhere in the semirural area around our house. We finally found out why vegetables kept disappearing from the kitchen. He was feeding them to the horse!

But there were other times when I was horrified. One day I saw my father putting the same brother's hands on the flames of the gas stove. This was my father's punishment for his taking some candy from a store near our house. It was normal that nobody ever talked about what happened. I didn't have the ability yet to put words to my experiences and observations, but my father's behavior felt incomprehensible, brutal. I felt sad and angry. I wanted to know what fed my father's capacity to do these monstrous things. An intense curiosity about such things began brewing inside.

❊❊❊❊❊❊❊❊

My tenth year was an exciting time. I found myself standing in front of my parents' shiny chestnut bedroom chest mirror, proudly feeling like a lady looking at myself wearing my mother's lipstick and high heel shoes. I also had a new school, and to my delight it was located in the heart of the city, which obliged me to take public transportation. I was in heaven. Here was proof that I was becoming a grown-up with new responsibilities and independence.

Before leaving the house to go to school, I made sure my hair was nicely done and my uniform skirt folded at the waist to be presentable. I liked the idea of being away from home. I loved listening to people around me in the bus and looking through the windows to the world outside. But I was frustrated because I often missed my bus, and because of this, I got to school late, and that lead to punishments. I would be made to kneel alone in the middle of a school courtyard with a couple of books balanced on my head and in sight of all my classmates. I hated becoming the center of attention in this negative way. I felt humiliated and greatly ashamed being the butt of ridicule. Never before had I had a discipline problem. Disconcerted, I was very unhappy with myself.

No one realized that I was late because I couldn't read the bus's route number in time to get on before it quickly moved away. No one noticed or found it strange that I always sat in the front row in the classroom squinting at the blackboard or that my nose was always buried in a book.

I thought nothing about feeling different and somewhat disconnected from others. I was beginning to learn that my new life, even with simple things, also had its difficulties, and I was finding out that my parents weren't the only ones who lacked any sense of the obvious in their world of unconscious violence.

I also didn't notice that in the photo taken of me at school, the word "America" was included in the school's name (above right), and there was a map of the world in the background, two pieces of information that were prescient in my spiritual journey.

❋❋❋❋❋❋❋❋

One afternoon after school, my father hastily came into the house fuming and shouting at my mom and me, "Get in the car!" I felt afraid and was reluctant to go, but I was learning there was no saying, "no" to my father. Trembling, I got into the car. He began crazily racing through the streets through neighborhood after neighborhood, and then through small towns around the city. I was asking, "What happened?" At some point my father, in what I had been learning was his usual angry and filthy language that made me not want to ask any questions, told me my brother had escaped home. I thought that things, painful things, must had happened between my father and my brother that made him leave home. But I wasn't aware of anything particularly bad.

My father stopped here and there, and every time we got out of the car, I was shocked walking among homeless people who were lying on the streets warming themselves with coverings of newspapers. Repeating what I saw my father doing, I uncovered one face and then another looking for my brother. My heart sank seeing this spectacle of human misery. I had never seen this before, and I felt very upset.

I couldn't believe I was searching for my brother among the homeless. In my mind I was asking myself, "Is this a dream? Is it my brother's new life to live in these terrible conditions?" And at the same time, sensing my father's fury, I quietly prayed for him not to be successful in finding my brother. My prayers were heard. We returned home empty-handed.

A few days later, though, when I came back from school, I found my brother chained to the floor and eating from a bowl like a dog. I was speechless and feeling helpless to change anything. I went numb.

I don't know how, but my father found my brother, and I heard from others that on the way home, my father gave him a tremendous beating. A few days later, my brother couldn't see in one eye. For years thereafter, my parents sought out medical assistance to no avail. My brother was to be blind in one eye for life. My worst fears had materialized. I was broken-hearted.

Their struggle continued, and one day my brother left home for good. His leaving was my loss. He was my favorite brother. We both liked to dance, and we had participated in TV shows receiving accolades for our presentation of folkloric dances. I loved his artistic sensitivities. He could draw, paint and was learning to sculpt. We had some contact once in a while, but as the years passed our relationship grew more and more distant.

My repressed anger grew toward my father for his brutality and my mother for her hard-heartedness in approving my father's behavior toward her children just to keep him near her. But I couldn't express any of this to anyone. There was no one in the family to turn to for support, and no one outside felt close enough to trust. If, improbably, there were social services for this kind of situation in those days, I wasn't aware of them or gave any thought to it.

✳✳✳✳✳✳✳✳

My father retired in his mid-forties from the job he was forced to take at fourteen when his father abandoned him and his mother. She was still a fairly young woman, and she never worked or created a life for herself. My father worked for a textiles plant, an important industry in its day, and became a self-taught mechanic capable of assembling huge machines bought overseas without the use of manuals or schematics. This showed to me that he was smart.

Someone in the company became aware of his technical acumen and offered him a move to work in the company's plant in the United States. But because of his mother's dependency on him from the time her husband left, he rejected the offer. My guess was that my father couldn't see leaving her behind in Colombia to fend for herself. He was to bitterly regret this decision the rest of his life.

My father eventually retired with the dream of becoming a farmer and soon bought a farm near a small village located about three hours from Bogotá, where we lived. I don't know about my brothers' adolescent dreams, but they, for sure as city boys, resisted my father's pressure to join him working on the farm. My father's control issues went through the roof, and all hell broke out. My two other brothers wound up leaving home and going in different directions. From then on, my father blamed them for any failings. They became my father's worst enemies. But very recently I heard that bedridden and near his death, he confided to a family member that he loved his sons.

After my brothers were gone, my mother's maternal instincts would periodically kick in, but my father always stopped her from seeing her sons. Her emotional distance was as wide and deep as the widest and deepest ocean. With no captain and no compass, my family's ship began sinking. I began gulping for air in the same immense roaring ocean of painful emotions.

****

I went to live with my parents on the farm. Our new house was seated on the top of a hill. It was tiny and made out of mud walls. It had a dirt floor in the kitchen and no running water or electricity. But I found something very charming about it. I liked gathering wood to cook and lighting the candles at night. Something about it suited my loneliness.

I delighted in walking around the farm and seeing big vistas. I loved taking cold showers from the huge tank that my father, very creatively, installed to collect rainwater that we used for all of our needs. I loved the open area in front of the house that he converted into a sort of a gazebo that became our living room. I loved this big and open space that invited nature in.

My mom enrolled me at a school in the nearest rural town. In traveling back and forth to it, I again often missed the bus and ended up walking the four miles through the countryside to school. Walking alone, I found moments when I felt alive in ways I didn't know were possible, moments when I could feel the air caressing every cell in my body. I discovered the sky. It was full of promise. When it rained, I felt both miserable and alive at the same time, and I was embarrassed when I arrived at school with muddy shoes and a spoiled uniform. Still, there was something great about being alone and totally immersed in the elements.

We had a few cows, and there was one that took a liking to my father. One day my father jokingly compared my dreamy eyes to those of the cow, and it was as if the cow heard and understood him, becoming quite jealous of me. Every time I came near it, it would charge me and try to knock me down. It was so funny. I was both entertained and puzzled.

One night I awoke to feel something crawling over my body. And then I heard my parents screaming because they were having the same experience. It was an army of ants that was on its way who knows where, and our home was in their way. Luckily for us, they didn't stop to bite us! It took them several hours to get through our house. I felt exhilarated, sensing the passing of what must have been millions of ants. I could feel energy flowing through and around us. This was a feeling of awe and wonder I would never forget.

In my walks around the farm, I encountered another place where I sensed this energy and felt in communion with nature and its forces. It was at a waterfall. I often went there alone and sat under it and felt the power of the water heal my body, mind, and heart. There my soul found solace. I didn't know that I was experiencing the life-giving vibrant energy that permeates all forms of life.

****

One day on my way to school, I met an intelligent and charming boy. I was a reserved thirteen-year-old girl, and he was an outgoing fifteen-year-old and son of the most influential family in town. I was aware that he was quite popular with the girls, and I felt privately proud he chose me as his girlfriend.

Sunday was my favorite day as my parents' routine was to go grocery shopping, which I loved to do as well. My father would park his car, and with my mother at his side, they would go into a store where they sold beer. They were there for hours talking with friends. Meanwhile my boyfriend snuck into the car, and we would spend time together talking while staying attuned to any movement that could indicate my parents were returning. Luckily, we were never found out. But I knew we were taking a chance and playing with fire.

Uncharacteristically, one Sunday my parents sent me alone to the village to buy our groceries. Naturally I loved the idea. My boyfriend and I shopped together as slowly as possible, stopping here and there to chat with our friends. Then I took a bus to go back home. I gave the groceries to the driver's assistant for him to put them in the bus's storage area as I boarded the bus. The bus was chock full, and when the time came for me to get out, there was a lot of chaos, and I couldn't get my grocery bags before the bus zoomed off.

My heart began pounding heavily, practically coming out of my chest. Things at the farm had gone from bad to worse. The precious plants I saw my parents worked so hard to plant were killed by freezing rains, and their chicken farm failed with a deadly contagious disease that eventually killed all the birds. Right then and there, I realized we had become poor. I saw in my mind's eye my parents collecting what pennies they had that morning for me to buy the groceries.

Panicking, I took a bus back into town, and my feet took me right to my boyfriend's house. It made sense. There wasn't anyone else I could reach out to. The person who greeted me was a tall and handsome man. I recognized him. He was my boyfriend's father. I hesitated for a second to speak. My hands were sweating, yet I knew I had no other recourse but to tell him what had happened to me. He listened intently and immediately reached into his pocket and kindly gave me money saying, "Don't worry. Go buy the groceries."

"Thank you, thank you very much," I said gratefully. My whole body was shaking as I walked out, holding back tears of shame and gratitude. What a loving man, I thought. But at the same time, I felt embarrassed and wanted to disappear from the face of the planet.

I moved quickly, rebuying the groceries and boarded the first bus I could to go home. All the way there, I was wracking my brain trying to figure out the best way to tell my story to my parents to cushion what I thought would be my father's sure punishment. I had been away for a long time, and the new grocery bags would give me away. When I finally got home, I found myself telling my parents what had happened to me exactly the way it did.

My father was furious. His pride was hurt, and he began shouting at me, "SOB. Don't you have any shame? How could you go there begging for money? What a disgrace!" I felt ashamed of myself for having caused this embarrassing and painful situation, and I was surprised that my father didn't hit me physically.

A few days later, I was surprised when my father came home fuming and shouting at me, "What are you thinking? He is a *nobody*—a clown with no future." He was talking about my boyfriend, and it was obvious to me that my father had already lined up some insults for him. Did my father even know that I was dating him? But apparently my father had heard some gossip that there were preparations for me and this boy to get married and that a rich aunt was offering him land and money to build us a house. I knew nothing about any of this. But this was the end of my life on the farm. My father sent me back to live in our house in Bogotá.

****

Despite all the problems, living on the farm was a time when nature whispered to my soul in so many ways about its mysteries and wonders. Spirit allowed me to catch a glimpse of the creative divine embedded in nature, and that I was a part of it all. I felt blessed by my experiences there. I discovered new places I could visit within whenever I wanted to. I often went there to consider what I saw happening to my family and my place in it.

I was dismayed seeing my parents' failed efforts, and somehow to me this had something to do with our family's disharmony. Something inside me understood that my father's anger derailed his powerful creative energies into deadly control issues. In my musings, I could envision and feel a beautiful world and wondered what kept my father from going to that place within. What kept him living in emotional negativity?

****

Back in Bogotá, I soon got immersed in all sorts of new routines including going to a school my mom, still showing interest in my education, found for me. I liked being back in the city and away from my father. I again felt a sense of liberation.

In my new life I met the tenants who occupied what used to be some of my living space. They were mostly women, and they became the older sisters and friends I never had growing up. My parents came from time to time to collect the rent and to check on what was left of the family, me.

My boyfriend began coming to the city to visit, wanting to continue our relationship. I, inexplicably, wanted nothing to do with him. He kept trying, but not really knowing what made me reject him, I was nonetheless firm about my decision. I didn't know there would be emotional residue from this situation, which I would have to deal with at a much later time when I was already married.

****

One day, following my teacher's advice, my mom took me for an eye exam, and after examining my eyes, the ophthalmologist asked me, "How have you been able to survive this long without glasses? You have an extreme congenital myopia for which you could have been declared legally blind." At sixteen, I was dumbfounded and had no answer. Of course, I couldn't even read the bus line number. Of course, I felt different and distant from others. For sure this impediment, I believe, obliged me to focus on the emotional to understand me, people, and situations. I became an empath who ironically was born and lived in a family environment simmering in the emotional silence that reigned in my father's kingdom of fear.

My mom ordered my first pair of glasses and, oh boy, I saw a whole new world before my eyes! Everything looked bright and glowing in a way I didn't know was possible. I discovered that seeing was exciting and invigorating, and it felt miraculous. The world was so rich and I was in it. I felt like I was being born again!

Seeing the world visually for the first time was magnificent, but looking at myself in the mirror was a different story. Another reality hit me. My glasses had coke bottle lenses. My adolescent vanity was challenged. I looked ugly with small, beady eyes.

Fortunately, my mom also didn't like how I looked in those glasses. As soon as she could, I can only imagine through a great deal of effort given that we now were poor, she bought me my first pair of contact lenses.

My self-esteem soared. I began to know that I liked me, and to feel comfortable in my skin. And, most importantly, I found that I loved life. I loved the life that I could see, peering into people's eyes, the mirror of their souls. I saw distinct shapes and colors in nature and the stars in the sky I didn't know existed because my eyes couldn't see them before. My teacher and my mother, no doubt, were angels. They had brought heaven to my doorstep! Somewhere within me, I felt my mother loved me.

My life had changed again. Inspired by this new world and the new me that my eyes saw, I started to really get moving in the game of life. I put aside any thoughts about the negative implications my visual handicap might have caused.

My newfound confidence began showing some results. Remembering my teacher's advice from the time when I performed well in a play at the school near my parents' farm (I had enjoyed the experience and kept this thought in back of my mind for a long time), I luckily found a theater school near my regular school and it happened to be the best one in the country. I asked for and was given an appointment to see the director. He interviewed me, and my nervousness disappeared as I, full of conviction, succeeded in getting across to him my clear objectives for speaking with him. I wanted to become an actress. I went through a very rigorous selection process and couldn't believe it when I heard that I was accepted. It felt so good to produce positive results out of my own intuition.

I began taking classes after school. One day in class, I was seated on the floor doing some body exercises when I lifted my head and my eyes met my father's red and angry face as he stared at me. He had come from the farm and went to my regular school where he did not find me. My classmates there directed him to go to the theater school.

"Oh, my god!", I exclaimed. In an instant I saw nothing but misery coming my way. He looked around at my classmates disapprovingly. They were the creative 60s types with long hair and round spectacles. Fuming with rage, he found his way to me, grabbed me by my ponytail, and began pushing and kicking me along the floor out into a small courtyard to the street and into his car. My scalp and body hurt and so did my pride—I felt disgraced. I was ready to die right then and there. In my mind I just disappeared from myself.

Once we were in the car, he began a litany of his filthy language, which by now was quite familiar and disgusting for me to hear. "SOB. So, you have decided to become a prostitute around those drug addicts," he said. Then making matters worse, he noticed I was wearing nylon stockings, and this infuriated him even more. Pinching my leg, he said, "What right do you have to make this kind of decision?" Then he proceeded to lay a guilt trip on me saying, "Oh, dear God, tell me what I have done to deserve this?"

When we got home, he slapped me again and again. Still furious, he took his belt off and began whipping my body. I felt like he was unloading all his pent-up emotions onto my body, eternally buried emotions that he desperately wanted to get rid of. The physical pain was unbearable. I thought he was going to kill me.

I don't know what made him stop, but he left me lying on the floor. When I could finally move again, I took myself to bed where I fell into a sort of hibernation. I couldn't and *didn't* want to get up.

My troubles as my father's adolescent daughter had just begun. I knew what I was up against regarding him and his ways, and right then and there, I must have made a commitment to myself that I would dedicate my life to gathering all the inner strength I could muster to remain alive and well forever. My father was not going to beat this will out of me.

My father went back to the farm, and I sadly never went back to the theater school. I blocked out thoughts of the public spectacle my father had made of me there. I continued my regular school classes as if nothing happened, just like I saw my parents do after their fights. I also never talked about this with my mother or anyone else. I put my dream to become an actress aside, never to dwell on it again. I knew the black and blue marks from my father's beating were bound to heal and disappear—and so would the stains on my pride. But it would take a long time. Guided by the hands of Spirit, the spiritual warrior in me had been *awakened,* and I was beginning to confront the fear that has consumed civilizations for eons!

****

Without the words to put to my own emotions, I was lost in my own world. Often when others wanting to really know me asked, "What are you thinking about?" I never knew what to answer.

I couldn't tell them I was mentally talking with friends I had met a long time ago, perhaps even from a previous life —silence, solitude, faith, and trust. Conversing with them while gazing at the sky, I kept on trying to understand the nature of my family's dynamics, my father's rage, my mother's emotional distance and submissiveness towards my father, my brothers' abandonment by my parents, my role in this life, and, most importantly, where did I really come from and for what purpose? These were things that occupied my existence. But I barely could verbalize them to myself.

Meanwhile, living with my parents, I encountered polarities that obliged me to search for my inner core. A lot had to do with the crudeness of my father's attitude and behavior and my mother's approval of it. One day, for example, when I saw my mother joining my father in throwing our garbage all over the roof of the house of a family that had taken over an open space next to our home, every fiber within me was repugnant at their act. I didn't want anything to do with this sort of vicious behavior.

* * * * * * * *

Every year I grew more discouraged facing the reality that, academically, I was so far behind my classmates that there was no way I was going to be able to graduate from high school. Intuitively, something was telling me that I could buy more freedom from my father's authoritarian rule if I earned my own money. One day, I made my decision. One year before finishing high school, I dropped out to find a job.

Searching in the newspaper want ads, I followed a lead that landed my first job as a sales assistant at an optical shop. This was so exhilarating to me! I felt that the world's doors were opening for me and for once, I *knew* I had choices. In the optical shop there were all sorts of colored lenses and frames at my disposal to browse and to help others to see their World. I didn't see it then, but what a perfect metaphor for my situation. *Spirit was at work.*

When I was nineteen, my parents finally came back from the farm heartbroken and bankrupt. Farm life proved difficult for them. The climate of the farm's zone wasn't appropriate for growing the strawberries for export my father had envisioned.

Trying one thing after another became much more expensive than my parents realized. To pay their debts, my father sold his mother's home in the city and brought her to live with us on the farm. She had a stern personality and character and like my parents—the tone of our relationship was distant and cold. She passed away while living with us on the farm.

After a year or so, my parents had a mess on their hands. On top of everything, they came back expecting my mom's fifth child. Her previous baby, me, had come nineteen years earlier.

One day I received a phone call at my office to let me know that my mom was taken to the hospital deathly ill with a serious case of eclampsia—a disorder of pregnancy. I didn't know she was pregnant—nobody did!

The baby was suddenly brought into the world at seven months, and my mother was physically okay. But she later developed a chronic depression that became the cause of a future attempted suicide. I never could discover why my mom chose to hide her pregnancy in the first place, but deep inside my gut, I understood her dilemmas. It seemed like the jumble of powerful emotions from excitement and joy to the fear and anxiety her pregnancy may have caused, and their weight of emotions took a toll on her. I wished I could have helped her, but I knew I couldn't change anything about her suffering. Sadly, I could only be a firsthand witness.

※※※※※※※※

In retrospect, my intuition to drop out of school and get a job was timed perfectly. With my small salary, I offered my parents and my little brother support. Doing so was a steppingstone to gain some independence from my father's rule. Striking out on my own financially gave me more confidence to own my decisions and to create my own social environment.

While meeting people of my choosing, I met Miguel Angel, a true angel beyond just his name. He was a close friend of the optical shop owner. Our friendship would be significant in my life in more than one way. To begin with, he helped me enroll in a technical school where, while working full time during the day, I prepared at night to become an executive administrative assistant. I was being practical, and my goal was to increase my earning power. He liked me, and he thought that one day we would be more than friends. I disagreed.

Meanwhile, my soul's yearnings kept on nagging at me. I found solace focusing on trying to figure out more about the sense of the divine and fear I felt while living on the farm and when I looked into other people's eyes. I had little support and guidance about the practical aspects of my life, but my inner life was rich, intense, and focused. While my mind went crazy trying to make sense of my experiences, and I felt lost in the physical world, an invisible thread was guiding my existence and I delighted in it. Doing my soul's work was so important that everything else paled in comparison—including living with an abusive father—which I dealt with as well as I could. But my spiritual endeavor was what really mattered.

And as I began walking the spiritual path in earnest, one day I realized that I wasn't finding anything particularly meaningful by attending church. Without any drama about my decision, I stopped going. I simply left organized religion.

For a lot of my life up to this point, I had a sense there was something higher or bigger than the day-to-day human experience. The word "God" would appear in my consciousness, and I would look up into the sky looking to see if I could find her. I wanted to know more, a lot more about this. I began reading philosophical books like *Jonathan Livingston Seagull, The Little Prince, Demian, Siddhartha, Leaves of Grass,* and *The Art of Living*. I took a class at the Colombian Institute of Parapsychology. There were so many inexplicable things in life. I went out with others exploring places thought of as energy vortices. I thought maybe I could find what moved an army of ants and what fed my father's rage. Two inexplicably different forces!

On one field trip with a group of parapsychology students, I went to the beautiful Laguna de Guatavita, which is a sacred lake at the bottom of an extinct volcano about 35 miles north of Bogotá. Many centuries ago, Muisca Native Americans conducted a ritual where the chief, covered in gold dust, ventured out on a ceremonial raft to the middle of the lake where he dove into the water, washing off the gold dust as an offering to the Gods. This legend is the basis for the widely known legend of El Dorado.

We hiked to the top of the volcano where there was an unusual and large circular spot made of powdered sand. Nothing grew there, and yet all around it was abundant vegetation. The idea was that an extraterrestrial object had landed there leaving a mark, and we were there to channel the energy of the place. For sure, I thought, there must be other forms of life somewhere that are similar to human life.

A deeper sense of inquiry and contemplation was manifesting in my daily life. This would be my first instinctual action to explore the ways of my ancestors.

Unfortunately, this unique experience ended for me when the organizers wanted the participants to give them a percentage of our earnings. Was it a cult? I thought so and ran away, quickly!

****

Still, the practicalities of life also mattered to me, and seeking a better salary, I moved from job to job and eventually found myself working for governmental agencies such as the Colombia National Department of Planning and the Foreign Commerce Institute. These agencies, as their names indicate, were charged with developing and implementing social and economic policies for the country.

In these jobs I found myself absorbed in learning all that I could from the material I handled as a secretary and from conversing with the highly educated people around me. This was like finding water by someone dying of thirst. In my mind, I secretly and desperately wanted knowledge, and intuitively I began extracting all that I could from such a rich work environment.

Many of those around me had degrees from top universities in the U.S. and Europe and were bringing economic theories academically developed into their work. I shared with them that I saw a disconnect. I was worried and wanted to understand how economic theories conceived abroad could possibly address the realities of people's lives in Colombia.

The world of international politics also interested me, and I avidly consumed the newspapers' international sections. I remembered admiring John F. Kennedy from the time when he and his wife, Jackie, visited Bogotá when I was a young girl. But now, I had misgivings about the level of influence I observed the U.S. government had in the internal affairs of Colombia. But despite my misgivings, I had fun participating in Bogotá's version of the Woodstock Festival where people of my age dressed like hippies and sang and danced to music I couldn't really understand.

One day I was quite surprised when I was wishing one of my bosses a farewell. He was taking a post at an overseas international agency, and out of the blue, he said to me, "I see you also abroad." I thought to myself, "What is he possibly talking about?" I certainly wasn't dreaming about going overseas, much less living abroad. But Spirit was announcing something that my ears were not yet ready to hear—much less understand.

✳✳✳✳✳✳✳✳

I continued working and attending school, and on Fridays I joined the cultural tradition of going out with friends or a prospective boyfriend, dining, and dancing. During those days I still had to ask my father's permission to come home later than usual.

Dancing became the only thing in my life that helped me escape, and so I often went past the curfew hour, knowing that my father would be waiting up for me to slap and verbally insult me for being late. At some point though, I began challenging my father with questions like, "What else do you want from me? I am a mature woman in my twenties. I am being responsible, working, studying and helping you, my mom and my little brother financially." He had no answers.

Curiously, throughout this time of contention with my father, the thought of leaving home never, ever occurred to me as it was typical in my culture for unmarried women to remain living at home. I was quite resourceful otherwise, and I chose to be happy while dancing. But, I was always anxious on the way home and depressed the next day or so.

Little did I know then that in my spiritual path, playing the role of a witness would be critical for me to experientially know and understand the nature of, and the antidote to, human suffering. Living with my father, not letting his abusive behavior break my spirit, was indeed an essential step that, with the help of Spirit, I *could* handle. I didn't know a day would come when this would lead me to leave home for good.

In the meantime, I was a young and, my friends would say, an attractive woman with a friendly disposition, intellectually engaged who wanted to find but was pitifully failing in finding the right person to be romantically involved with in a meaningful way. I had plenty of admirers, and it became almost a routine for me—dating and searching for someone I was truly interested in, and men continuously disappearing from my life. It made me particularly sad to think that perhaps my family's low socioeconomic status was what deterred them.

What made me think this way was the experience around a romantic relationship when my heart was first broken. Guillermo, a naval officer from Bogotá, belonged to a family from a higher socioeconomic status than mine. He suddenly disappeared but showed up again a couple of years later. We became good friends. Eventually, he was getting married, and I happily accepted his invitation to the wedding. The reception was taking place at a five-star hotel in Bogotá, and I invited a male friend to accompany me to the party. We showed up elegantly dressed for the occasion, and I was stunned when the groom and his sister—the only people I knew in the family—acted as if they didn't know me. Others in the family wondered who my friend and I were, and we were politely asked to leave. I was so embarrassed, and my heart began to hurt again. This experience was very telling to me about the role of social status in our society.

Hiding in the pain of that experience was my not realizing that I was my own worst enemy because I couldn't share of myself, even with my girlfriends. I didn't realize that I, like my parents, was emotionally handicapped. *My heart was closed.*

This affected the Friday after work outings, and I was often left in pain, feeling confused, rejected, and depressed. I began reacting with crying spells, and all I could think was, "What is going on with me?" Following my friends' advice, I found some relief treating my symptoms of unhappiness by drinking hot milk laced with brandy. I guess I hoped my problem was physical. I didn't realize that I was facing the challenge to live and love with a closed and broken heart.

****

The boyfriend I had on the farm moved to Bogotá to pursue his college studies. By then it was clear we were going to be just friends, and from then on, I only saw or heard from him on my birthday. We would have fun together dining and, of course, dancing.

I hadn't seen him for a while when one day I received a phone call from one of our mutual friends with awful news. He was taken to a hospital with a terrible headache. The doctors found out he had a brain tumor that needed to be removed immediately, but he passed away right before having the surgery. He was only in his early twenties and was within days of becoming an engineer and getting married.

Shocked, I immediately went to his funeral in his town. I was impressed to see that the cathedral where the service was taking place was totally full. He obviously had a lot of friends who, like me, were moved by his generous and warm personality and took his death as a terrible tragedy.

I was a bit surprised when after the service, his mother invited me to come to their house. I was taken aback when she took me to his bedroom. On the nightstand on one side of his bed, she showed me an old photograph of me. I felt very sad realizing what he felt for me, and that I probably had caused him pain. But I felt gratitude for all that my life on the farm had given me. Memories like this from my life at my parents' farm would surface again, but not before a couple of life-changing events.

❉❉❉❉❉❉❉❉

One late afternoon just before Christmas, I came out of my office building and saw a group of children playing in the street and bathing in a public fountain. They appeared to be lost in their world, swimming and splashing water all about. I saw adults passing them by, carrying Christmas presents for their own children. And as the multicolored lights celebrating the happy season illuminated the scene, they suddenly also illuminated my mind, causing me to wonder about those children in the fountain. I asked myself, "Where are *their* Christmas gifts?" I saw how separated these children were from the children for whom parents bought presents. I had seen homeless children before, but this time I saw them with the new eyes of my soul.

I suddenly found myself doing a little shopping. All the way to the store, I kept imagining different ways I could ask for help. Once I was in front of the manager, something made me tell him what I had seen and my desire to do something about it. Being honest like this felt like the time when, feeling out of control, I asked for money to buy the groceries I had lost, and then telling my parents exactly what had happened to me.

I was learning that being honest was one way to deal with fear, fear of being punished, rejected, neglected, shamed, and blamed. I saw that being honest touched on the limitations of the human experience. I had no business spending the little money I had on gifts for the children when there were needs back at home. I said to the store manager, "The truth is, I don't have much money to go shopping like this, but I would like to help those children."

I walked out of the store full of packages—gifts from the manager—feeling like "the happiest person in the whole world." All the way back to the fountain, in my mind's eyes, I saw the faces of the store's manager, the children, and me happily blended together. I was relieved to see that the children were still there, and I sat on the side of the fountain as the children surrounded me as I gave each one a Christmas gift. Their little eyes shone like brilliant stars. Mission accomplished. I cried, feeling gratefulness, joy, and love.

I knew this moment was different from my normal reality. Here, an awareness kicked in, and I wasn't myself. My mind and body became instruments of a *force,* an energy that activated them in concert for a particular goal. Again, was this the same energy that moved the army of ants at the farm? In other words, I knew "I" didn't go to the store. My feet took me there, and my mind followed along from the fountain to the store and back again. I was sure Spirit talked through me to the store manager. This was so refreshing, even though when I came back to myself, I was painfully aware of the normal lives of those homeless children.

****

And there was another time when my whole world was shaken up. On a Sunday during the "season" in Bogotá, I dressed up in my best clothes with anticipation for the spectacle awaiting me. I was going to be taken to a *corrida de toros,* a traditional bullfight. Almost every year a dear friend invited me to this event, and I looked forward to being part of the crowd and its huge array of men's and women's fashions.

When we arrived at the plaza de toros, the actual bullring, it was full of euphoria, glamour and festivity—just like so many other afternoons that I enjoyed in years past. It was sunny with a delightful light breeze. Everything promised that it was going to be a great afternoon.

The band's music invaded the air, the sun shone on our faces, and the scent of Manzanilla-sherry began permeating our senses. The bugle sounded, and the roaring crowd began cheering the bullfighters and their assistants. They entered the bullring in all their splendor of bright and multicolored tight outfits. Even their horses were delightfully dressed. The arena was alive with anticipation for the ritual to follow.

The first bull, a magnificent, huge, and beautiful creature, jumped out into the light of the bullring, snorting and kicking. His monumental presence and his energy matched the emotions of the crowd. It seemed like it fed off of our energy. Or was it the other way around?

The bull brimmed with life. As expected, the picador used his lance to test the bull's strength, draw the first blood, and force his head lower, preparing him for the set of barbed sticks placed by the *banderilleros* that further wounded and agitated the bull and prepared it for the last part of the ritual when the toreador does his cape work before driving a sword into the bull's neck.

Everyone was clapping to the well-done job of the picadors. The noise reached a deafening crescendo in my ears, and suddenly my eyes focused on the river of blood running down the bull's body. My heart pounded hard and my whole-body shivered. Full of horror, inconsolable tears suddenly began flowing from my eyes down my face, and unsuccessfully fighting them back, I began running—running away from the bullring and such a horrendous spectacle.

I felt stronger and more fluid. I didn't know that in leaving the plaza, my body and mind were surrendering to my soul's outrage. My soul repelled the murder of the bull for the sole purpose of human entertainment. I now understood that *the bull was the divine expression of the energy of life.* My sensibilities toward the sacredness of life were growing, and this meant there was an awakening process taking place. It also meant that my soul had limits.

Spirit was by my side guiding each of my steps, one by one, giving me the opportunity to identify from my experiences the lessons that could offer me clues to my inner quest. Paying attention, listening to my own emotions was key, and so was choosing my decisions. I chose to end what had become a tradition for me. I never attended a bullfight again. Something in me was changed.

✱✱✱✱✱✱✱✱

Looking for a meaningful experience of life, I, directionless for years, had been jumping around, taking university level classes in computers, economics, business administration, and social communications, but never settling on a discipline. I equated my desire for knowledge with becoming a qualified professional. I didn't know that there were different paths to knowledge, and that I was nurturing a lifelong desire for learning.

One day my frustration peaked, and I found myself growing the courage to finally look myself in the mirror and face the root of the paralysis that had become a main obstacle in realizing my thirst for knowledge. I acknowledged that I needed to validate my high school studies by taking the national test (something like the GED in the U.S.), and that I was terribly afraid of failing it. Once I made up my mind, I passionately applied myself to preparing for the test.

I was elated and felt proud and free like never before seeing my name on the list of those who passed the test. Nobody, not even me, knew how significant passing this test was in my life. Maybe if I went to the Moon? It symbolized my finally getting over the huge emotional hurdle I had been harboring in my heart since my childhood, since the time when almost blind, I began performing poorly academically! Resolving to confront this fear was one of the greatest things I ever did in my life.

Little by little, I was taking steps that fed my spirit, and the more I did, the more opportunities presented themselves for me to exercise my determination.

I took a job from someone who knew me socially. This was another person in my life who saw above and beyond the physical and valued and trusted the content of my character and my skills. I felt so refreshed that he recognized in me the mature and reliable individual I was becoming as well as my people, communications, and organizational skills. He hired me as the director of public relations, managing a continuing education program for architects and engineers at an urban research center under the auspices of the Colombia National University.

After about three successful years, I became restless, wanting more than this job could offer me. I followed my intuition and quit without knowing what was next. Something inside—a little voice was saying I was about to commit to a fundamental change, perhaps even including getting married.

Oddly, my father and I were in sync about this, although for different reasons. He was concerned that at twenty-six, I was quickly becoming too old to be a candidate for marriage. And he was actively looking for a good prospect for me, which I think meant someone of economic means. I knew I was ready to open my heart to trust somebody and embrace a stable, loving, and peaceful relationship. Whether the person was of financial means or not was not something that concerned me. And I didn't know that I was also ready to do what had been unimaginable to me up until then—leave home.

Another friend, the one who believed that one day we were going to be romantically involved, was asking me to marry him. One day he dropped me off at home after a weekend outing with a group of friends when my father jumped out of the front door pointing his gun at my friend and shouting, "You must marry her, or I will kill you!" I firmly planted my feet on the ground and looked straight into my friend's eyes and asked him to leave.

Once inside the house, my father, assuming my friend and I had had an affair, screamed at me that I was "a disgrace to our family." To me whether we had an affair or not was none of my father's business. I was well aware that my parents liked him, and I saw my father's theatrics, acting out his machismo to force us to marry. Little did my father know that I had been considering to marry my friend, but that I'd arrived at the conclusion that I had no business marrying him because I was not in love with him.

When my boyfriend and I got together the next time, my heart opened like never before in my life. I said to him, "I am sorry, but I can't marry you. As I always have told you, I love you, but I am not in love with you." I also pointed out that no relationship could survive the toxicity of my family, and that we didn't deserve that kind of life.

He was quite angry and I knew a bit about the pain of feeling rejected. In my heart I understood his reaction. It was painful to be brutally honest. Yet, there was nothing that I could do differently. Our lives were precious, and I knew my truth was the only thing I had to go by.

This time my father's disrespect toward my dear friend and me with such a delicate matter touched my soul's limit. Ironically, my father who had fought me so feverishly was instrumental in my abandoning his drama. Leaving my parents' home was imminent—and my life was in Spirit's hands.

****

As I was finding my own direction, what at first seemed like a bad cold became a bout of depression so bad that for several days, I didn't want to talk to or see anyone. I didn't want to open the blinds in my bedroom because I didn't want to see the sunlight. I became afraid that I was losing my love of life.

I began connecting the dots between my more and more frequent and intense spurts of depression and the fact that to ease my symptoms, I had been increasing my intake of the brandy and milk. I saw a doctor who told me that I had hypoglycemia and that it needed to be treated because it could become diabetes. Intuitively, I was averse to starting a traditional medicine treatment, and I began looking for an alternative treatment.

TWO

Into the Light

Ecuador

I had been dating a man from the United States who I met at my last job. One day he asked me to marry him. He was moving to Quito, Ecuador, to take a job in the oil industry. In considering his proposal, I decided that I needed to visit him to get to know him better before making my final decision. I invited a girlfriend to come with me to Quito, the capital city.

Just before our arrival, he unexpectedly was called away to do his job on an oil pipeline in the jungle where he needed to be for the next three weeks, and he asked his friend John to host us. John and my boyfriend were both from Chicago and mutual friends of the person John had come to visit in Ecuador.

John greeted us at the airport, and from there we went to our hotel. We settled in and discussed a three-week vacation plan to fill the time until my boyfriend came back to Quito. We decided to visit one of the Ecuadorian beaches, and considering that none of us had much money, the three of us camped out in a tent. We were amused when in the morning the guys winked at John who had two ladies with him in a small tent. My girlfriend soon decided that camp life was not for her and went back to Bogotá. I thought nothing of staying alone with John, and we stuck with our plan.

We began to get to know more about one another in a simple way—but not without difficulties since our bilingual skills were rather non-existent. One night, for example, we were walking along the beach, and I felt the urge to urinate. I told John, "Necesito hacer chichi" "I need to pee," but he kept following me as we walked along. This sequence repeated a couple of times because he had no idea what "chichi" meant. I finally got it across to him with some rather crude sign language. Afterwards, we laughed our heads off thinking about it!

In our conversations I learned that John was passing through Quito after a journey through the Americas that had taken years. He was visiting an old friend before going to Burma where he had been accepted to join a Buddhist monastery. I'd grown interested in Buddhist philosophy, and I felt a spiritual connection to him. His words were strumming divine chords in my soul and mind.

Being in a foreign country on my own and sharing so much of my soul with another person I barely knew was quite new to me. But I was totally comfortable being myself in the company of a person who felt authentic and sincere.

At the end of the three weeks, John and I went back to Quito and met my boyfriend and a group of people who, for the most part, were foreigners from the United States and Europe. In the course of our conversations, we learned that among us there was a chiropractor, a masseur, a businesswoman, a businessman, John who knew about vegetarianism and meditation, and me with my communications skills. All of us were enjoying being in Ecuador, and the conversation soon was about putting our knowledge and skills into a joint venture. We could all stay in Ecuador and open a health clinic! A creative energy took over, and a few weeks later, we all moved into a large, ultramodern house we'd rented in a gorgeous suburban area in Quito.

This idea perfectly suited me. I was seeking an alternative life as well as a natural way to treat my bouts of depression. The little voice inside was telling me this was the right place for me, and I made my decision to stay for good. My life was changing by leaps and bounds, and I was experiencing fresh emotions and meaningful relationships.

Life was colorful and vibrant, and so was Ecuador and its people. I learned that about 80% of the country's population was indigenous, and I found myself particularly drawn to observing and admiring their cultures. Except for my exploration around Lake Guatavita, while living in Bogotá, I didn't have any awareness of these communities in Colombia.

A few months later, I needed to go back to Bogotá to pick up my belongings and to renew my tourist visa. John needed to travel outside of Ecuador to renew his visa as well. In my new freedom, I thought nothing of inviting him to travel with me and to stay with my parents while we were getting our visa extensions at the Ecuadorian Consulate in Bogotá.

Every night I found myself awake and nervously attuned to any sound that could indicate my father's ire, but all went well. My father, sensing that something had changed in our relationship, was unusually pleasant, and I was focused on pursuing my new life. My actions themselves were speaking loud and clear that I was by no means going to come back to live with my parents. My father's intuition was right. Indeed, something had fundamentally changed. What he couldn't see was that I had no doubt left home for good.

****

When John and I came back to Quito, I got a surprise. We found two new women living in our house. My prospective husband had invited a couple of British ladies he had met to live with us. Needless to say, this felt funny, and I soon knew the reason.

One evening we were having a party by the fireplace on the second floor of the very open atrium of our new house. I had left the group to take a nap, but soon changed my mind and decided to join the party again. I was coming downstairs from my bedroom, and my eyes couldn't believe what I saw. I blinked several times to make sure, but I was seeing my prospective husband passionately embracing and kissing one of the British girls. I came down, and he acted as if nothing was going on. Afterwards, I confronted him about what I saw, and he said, "You didn't see anything. You were dreaming!" I was astounded that he was trying to convince me that I was just dreaming. His actions were all too familiar to me. He was a womanizer and a liar. I could never trust him again.

It wasn't hard for me to say to him, "Hasta la vista, baby," but he didn't believe me. He got really angry and acted out his rage, cutting up my bed with a knife and threatening to kill John. He thought John had influenced my decision to end our relationship. I abhorred his drama, and I saw through it and how manipulation and violence go hand by hand. This became a blessed opportunity for me to consciously choose that I wasn't ever going to walk in my parents' footsteps if I could help it. My life was going to be different.

Regardless, John and I left town for safety reasons and went traveling for a couple of weeks until things cooled down at home. It turned out that our other friends had a long talk with my now ex-boyfriend, basically threatening him. He calmed down and backed off.

John and I had a good time together and I began considering that all through our adventures together at the beach when I first met him, going to Bogotá as friends, and now traveling together, John was a gentleman, an honest person, and a good, enlightened soul. I delighted in his company. The barrier that had kept me locked in fear and distrust of others had begun to come down, and I wasn't afraid to open my heart to him. Period. I could never have imagined how huge this was to be in my life.

****

When John and I got back to Quito, we started a romantic relationship and moved in together. He dropped his idea of going to Burma. Sometime afterwards I jokingly said, "If you are looking for Nirvana. You have now found it." Nirvana was being with me! For the first time in my life, I had a sense of inner peace and joy!

John's tourist visa prevented him from getting a job. Because of Ecuador's treaties with other South American countries, I could get a job if I met a few requirements. Amazingly, while doing my research, I recognized the name of the Colombian consul in Quito. He was someone I knew from my government work in Bogotá. When I walked into his office, I was relieved that he remembered me. After some small talk, I told him I needed an official permit to work. He listened carefully and proceeded to calmly produce the paper. After thanking him, I confidently walked away and out into this new World to make a living.

I found a job at an international renewable energy agency. I felt blessed to be around people researching the application of alternative forms of energy like solar and biogas, and it didn't matter that I was a secretary again earning a small salary. I was happy like never before in my life. Did anybody notice? I had found my soul mate!

John became a homemaker by shopping, cooking, washing, and cleaning while I worked. We were happy living together. He was a vegetarian, and I needed no convincing about adapting new eating habits. My instincts about the negative effects of drinking brandy with hot milk to treat my bouts of depression were confirmed by a doctor who said there was a link between sugar consumption and depression.

From one day to the next, I radically eliminated consuming sugar, and the effects were almost immediate. John also gave me some herbal treatments and a strict vegetarian diet to eliminate what he thought were toxins in my body. On a physiological level, horrible sores opened on my face, arms and legs, discharging puss. I began to understand the effects of toxicity on the body, and there was a lot more I was about to learn.

One day John and I were at a movie theater when I felt distraught, and a tremendous torrential storm of emotions took me by surprise. I began sobbing nonstop; my tears felt like they were coming from an unknown place within. John helped me get out of the theater and we found a place to sit away from people, and he witnessed me pouring inconsolable tears for a long time. Something I saw in the film triggered a feeling that I was not my parents' daughter.

I'd never felt anything like this or even close to this before. There was an inner force pushing toxic emotions to the surface from the most ancient recesses of my heart. It was as if the crying had its own mind. Afterwards, I didn't have much to say or to think about the episode. In my memory I even forgot the title and plot of the movie we had been watching. But a profound peace followed and my bouts of depression disappeared. I stopped experiencing emotional ups and downs, and I felt the harmony my soul had desired for so long. I was beginning to experience the mind-body-heart connection. Not eating sugar and eating healthfully would prove to be a lifetime change. In the way of Spirit, the dream of opening an alternative health clinic was gone. Instead, I was experiencing my own healing.

※※※※※※※※

I liked living in Quito because it was smaller and more relaxed than Bogotá. Curiously though we ended up moving about six times during the couple of years we lived there. Somehow our conservative landlords found out we were not married and asked us to find new accommodations! I don't know how they discovered that. I was surprised by the property owners' attitude and behavior. It just didn't make sense to me that anybody would care that much about the private life of others.

I suppose that in retrospect, people may have seen me as being quite daring—living unmarried with a man. But I began to feel so clear and fluid about each new step I was taking. Unlike my father, I didn't think it was necessary that I marry, although I was certain that I wanted a meaningful relationship and felt in my heart that John was the right person.

Despite how I felt about it, I devised a strategy to smooth my relationship with my parents. I wanted peace in the family. Whenever I communicated with them, I referred to John as my boyfriend, implying that we lived in separate places.

****

Our life continued in Quito. We found the time to pay attention to the social environment around us and I learned that urban development was pushing indigenous communities to the higher mountainous regions around the city where it was difficult for them to grow crops. John and I talked about this, and we decided to explore helping the situation by addressing the nutritional needs of those communities. We thought we could do so by introducing people to cultivating soy as an inexpensive source of protein. John knew quite a bit about it, including how to make tofu.

We held a focus group with elders from a tribal community and followed up inviting them for a soy foods dinner to test their level of acceptance. It was a very well attended affair. The next day our landlord said, "This house does not welcome Indians." She essentially evicted us for the "heinous" act of trying to help people she (and some others in her social class) considered subhuman. The hands of Spirit were guiding me now to learn in a close and personal way about the prejudices that, above and beyond my blood family, clog the human experience.

****

My small salary barely kept us alive, and John's savings from his work years ago were drying up. We decided that we were going to move to the United States and get married. John would look for a job back in the computer industry after an absence of five years.

I told my parents about our plan, and we invited them to come to Quito for a vacation before going back together to Bogotá by car. There I would realize my dream of having a pre-wedding reception before departing for Chicago, John's hometown, to get married on my fiancé visa.

In preparation for their arrival, we arranged to have separate living conditions, but they arrived earlier than expected. My father acted cool, and we asked them to go to the beach while I finished my work responsibilities. They did, and on their return, we took off to Colombia in my father's car.

Once in Colombian territory, we stopped in Cali for a night at a friend's house. My mom had made this arrangement. Our families knew each other since our childhood, and the last time I'd seen my friend was when we took college-level classes together. She was now married, and she and her husband had lived in, of all places, Chicago where he pursued his PhD. They were eager to share their experiences with me; I was looking forward to it.

My father and her husband began to drink, and in short order, her husband began to say, "You are making a grave error.

Don't go to Chicago. It is terrible to live there." Apparently, they had been treated badly there.

The kind of chaos I knew so well around my father hopelessly unrolled before my eyes. His repressed ire about discovering we were living together in Quito exploded, and a litany of filthy language followed. In his eyes now, I, for sure, was "a prostitute who has dishonored the name of the family." He said that everyone in Bogotá was going to know that I had lived with a man without being married—a ridiculous statement for such a large city of some six million people at the time. Then he looked at John, and ignoring the fact that he was sick (he was quite ill with a fever, probably from the change of altitude and climate), my father began defaming me, telling John that it wasn't his fault, it was his daughter's, the prostitute's fault. Our plan to keep the usual drama out of my life was derailed.

Nothing about this was surprising to me. My father was very smart and manipulative, but I wasn't falling into his trap to force me to move back to their home. I resolutely stated to everyone, "I understand that you are saying these things to me because you care about me. I appreciate your efforts, but this is my life and I am conscious of the step I am taking."

John and I bought tickets for the earliest possible flight to Bogotá and left Cali and my family. In Bogotá we stayed with the girlfriend, who earlier had traveled with me to Quito, and her family until the time came for us to leave for the U.S. They lived in a new development whose roads were not yet paved. It started raining, the roads got muddy, and on the day we left, the taxi could barely make it out. Not at all an auspicious time to leave!

The day the plane took off from Bogotá's El Dorado airport with us on board to come to the United States, I got to feel a depth of emotional pain I didn't know was possible. The World was half-dark and half-light. I was very sad about the eternal state of my relationship with my parents. Nothing had ever changed about that. I hated to leave in these circumstances, and yet something inside told me I was doing the right thing. Why was there such a lack of harmony between us? Harmony is what I wanted in my life. I also felt sad that I couldn't have a beautiful and romantic pre-wedding ceremony in Colombia.

My heart was exploding into a million pieces, and yet I was happy to be with John. During the flight, and while making the connection to Chicago, the emotional contradictions moved little by little to the excitement of a new adventure.

I didn't know at the time that going to Ecuador was to signify the end of the first part of my life, a chapter where I experienced living amid fear. I would come to know that leaving to the U.S. was the beginning of a long and intense journey into a much larger World that had been foretold in that school photo and by the casual comment from my boss.

THREE

An Oracle Appears

The United States

In my first winter in Chicago, I played like a child with the fresh snow making angel wings. I felt like each snowflake descended from the sky to melt in my soul. I stood by the planetarium seeing the Chicago lakefront and its spectacular skyline shining on the shore of Lake Michigan, and I found myself weeping at the immensity of the view and the wondrous world that lay before me. All of these were exhilarating new experiences to me; it all felt divine.

When John asked me to come with him to the United States, I didn't hesitate for a second. I would go anywhere with him. Plus, I felt fully confident and excited about living in another foreign country. My adventuresome spirit was gleaming in joy. However, when I stepped out of the plane at O'Hare airport, an unexpected blow caught me off-guard. From one moment to the next, I lost my ability to understand what people were saying and to talk with them. I literally felt handicapped by my lack of English skills. The experience of living in Ecuador wasn't good at preparing me for this new reality.

With the exception of our landlords, in Ecuador I was treated with respect. Now in the U.S., interacting with people in an all Caucasian suburb and living with my mother-in-law in a neighborhood where nobody spoke Spanish, I felt the emotional weight of my new challenge. Some people would see my difficulties with English as though I were an "ignorant" person with no education and as though I had come from the jungle wearing a loin cloth and swinging from a tree. Some would raise their voices, thinking that by doing so, I would understand their English better as if I had a hearing problem. My mother-in-law even proceeded to teach me things like how to use the toilet!

It was kind of funny because as an adult, I understood what was going on, and not so funny because there was a wrong perception that gave way to attitudes and beliefs of which I was the brunt. I felt irritated that I couldn't share my mind with them. The World no longer looked so inviting. This time it was because I was aware that to others, I was invisible. This was awfully painful.

For a long while, my fiancé was the only person I could converse with. His Spanish skills, happily, kept on improving because of his practice with me. And my English slowly got better. In the learning process I began to understand what was being said a lot quicker than putting the words together to share my ideas. By the time I was ready to speak, the conversation had moved on. This was more than just frustrating—it was brutal.

Within three months of our arrival in Chicago, John and I got married. The ceremony took place on a Saturday in my mother-in-law's backyard. On the morning of the wedding, I opened my eyes and the blinds of my window to see a beautiful summer day full of promises. "Wow, I am getting married," I exclaimed to myself. If only my parents were here.

But the weather was changing. Rain was coming. I panicked and immediately turned to my mystical side, pleading, "Spirit, please take the clouds away." I lit candles to help the clouds evaporate. It worked—the rain went away.

A bit later under a luminous tree with John's family and friends, John and I were being caressed by a soft breeze. I was in heaven and in full gratitude. The minister pronounced a bunch of words I couldn't understand and really didn't care much about. Then at the end, I heard myself saying "I do." I loved saying I do and looking into John's heavenly blue eyes. Oh, how much I wished my parents had been there with us.

❊❊❊❊❊❊❊❊

I thrived in the intensity of my new life. It was challenging in terms of relating to others, and yet that void began being filled by an inexplicable inner buoyancy. So much had happened in such a short period of time.

Fortunately, an old friend, a living angel, found John a job again with a computer company. We really cut it close, though. When my husband got his first check from the new job, we were down to our last fifty dollars. Our lives had been saved—I felt Spirit was watching over us.

While he worked, my initial inspiration was to plant a vegetable garden, my first ever. All throughout the summer I gardened, working my small patch of land like my parents did on the farm. The work was difficult, yet the harvesting of anything I planted made it so worthwhile. I wished my parents could have experienced something so satisfying in their life on the farm.

I also began exploring possibilities in my new world. Most of what I saw of it was familiar— people being people, cities being cities. Politics, economy, social issues. I gained clarity about my earlier misgivings about the U.S., realizing that what I didn't like had to do with government policies—not people. But how I was perceived by others as different puzzled the heck out of me, and coming to grips with this would be an essential and lengthy passage.

As in my childhood and adolescent years, to survive, I was once again obliged to become quiet and observe. Earlier, I was visually handicapped in my family environment. Now I was linguistically handicapped living in this new culture. At times my life felt surreal and at other times, painfully real. Flashes of sadness would come but disappear as my friends, faith and trust, showed up, and I intuitively felt that all was well.

By the second year in Chicago, I was out and about, handicapped or not, exploring possibilities to get a job in places I'd spotted while we went out exploring the city's ethnic neighborhoods. Naturally, I opted to go first into the well-established, Spanish-speaking community in the inner city in Chicago. But I was dismayed to encounter that being a Spanish native speaker wasn't the asset I thought it was. Nobody knew me, and people there looked at me as if I came from another planet. This was really strange to me. In my new reality, I felt I was an outsider in both the English- and the Spanish-speaking communities! How could this be? I was disappointed and quite disconcerted. If I couldn't use my native Spanish skills, what else was I supposed to do to become a person again?

While I was trying to figure out this conundrum, I enrolled in a class to learn English and took on teaching myself to paint with acrylics. Eventually I had a couple of odd jobs to keep me busy. One of them was with a Spanish airline, which I quickly left when my manager sexually harassed me. Meanwhile, I was learning that there were opportunities assisting with the Spanish communication needs of local businesses and I began exploring them. On one occasion, for example, I sought to play a role in the coordination of a public relations campaign for Colombia. I took the initial steps, outreaching to influential people I knew back in Colombia, and even wrote a letter to and got a response from Colombia's president. The project didn't materialize, but I found it all interesting. I didn't realize I was an entrepreneur at heart in the making.

In our spare time, John and I enjoyed an active social life with friends and exploring the world of classical music and opera. With John as a guide and with the rich music culture in Chicago, that was easy. John had two degrees in music and was a member of the Chicago Symphony Chorus before he joined the corporate computer world. In Colombia I'd watched the Saturday opera programs as I cleaned the floors in our house. Music was always in the air for me! Dancing, though, was a whole different story. Initially my heart was excited to hear that we were going to a party, and then quite disappointed to learn that the get-together was just about people eating, drinking, and talking. There was no dancing; and to me, a party is not a party unless there is dancing. After a while I said to John, "We are going to a meeting, not to a party." Nevertheless, John introduced me to more of his friends, and some of them became my chosen family.

Going back to my family in Colombia, when my father saw pictures of our wedding, things got a bit better between us, and as soon as we could, we visited them. On that trip we went to the little town near where we had lived on the farm to visit my boyfriend's grave. For a long time, he kept showing up in my dreams. At his grave, I poured out my tears, explaining to him that I didn't mean to hurt him. I also pleaded with him to stop showing up in my dreams. When I came back home, my dreams about him mystically stopped.

****

By the third year in Chicago, with several seasons under my belt, I was beginning to understand the implications of a climatic environment that helped me better understand the differences in human behavior between those living in the north compared with those in the south. It was around simple things like how much energy and time it took me to just put on and take off coats, hats, gloves, mufflers, boots, and so forth in the Chicago winter; a season that doesn't exist in Colombia. It took a fair bit of planning to prepare to meet the elements and the seasons, something not needed in the warmer tropical climate I came from where it's mostly the same temperature year around, and it's either raining or not. Of course, the climate changes when you change elevation. Up it's colder; down it's warmer. That was true in my life in both Colombia and Ecuador.

I could see there are a lot of natural differences that, if not considered, become stereotypes that negatively affect our perceptions of one another and separate us. Because they have four seasons, people from the U.S. need to plan and think ahead. Therefore, they might be seen as calculating, yet cold. Because seasons do not present themselves in the tropics, people from the south can live more spontaneously, and might be seen as thoughtless, yet warm. All of this was so fascinating to me. I was just beginning to touch the surface in understanding cultural differences and stereotypes.

Eventually, I, and even my husband, a native Chicagoan, grew tired of the long, gray winter months, and we decided to move someplace else warmer. He saw an ad for a job in Raleigh, North Carolina, sent a letter of interest, got the job, and suddenly we had a new home. Spirit was at work again bringing about new opportunities.

I was excited. I knew that teaching Spanish was something I could do. Soon after our move to Raleigh, I had several private students. I began developing a program for executives and started working with a couple of corporate clients. Things were going very well and I opened a consulting firm. Between teaching and painting, my life was quite busy.

In 1986, on our first vacation trip within the United States, we went to visit the eastern indigenous pueblos of New Mexico. This was a further expression of the affinity we first felt with indigenous cultures when we met in Ecuador.

Initially, we visited a friend of my husband's from Chicago who was now living in Albuquerque. When she opened her front door as we embraced, my eyes saw a gorgeous turquoise and silver necklace (above) resting on the back of a couch in her spacious living room. I said, "Wow that is a quite a piece!" to which she replied, "Well, it is for you." She told us she was dealing in Indian jewelry and that the piece was for sale. Without asking many questions, we purchased it. Needless to say, I was delighted to own such a gorgeous piece.

After a few days we began traveling through the northern eighteen pueblos on the way to Taos. I wore the necklace, and I noticed that men in particular admired it saying, "Mighty, mighty powerful! Are you selling it?" It was obvious to me that they were admiring this object for more than its physical beauty. I was somewhat puzzled and left it at that.

I came back home with the necklace and a ceramic pot in the photo (below). I also came back with a kind of inspiration I had never felt before. I continued pursuing art, and I met somebody who taught me batik, an ancient wax resist art form. It became a means to somehow communicate when I couldn't with the spoken word. I created enough paintings to have a solo exhibit, which sold well. One of the batiks illustrated a dream where I was alone, sitting and meditating at a Kiva like the ones I had seen on that first trip to New Mexico. It was later bought by one of my clients for hanging in their corporate headquarters.

Every time I walked into the office where it hung, I felt a pang in my heart. I shouldn't have sold it, I kept telling myself. Years passed, and one day someone from the company called me asking if I wanted the painting back. Their office was closing for good. My soul was delighted to have it back. Ah, the ways of Spirit.

These three objects—the necklace, ceramic pot, and batik—were to have significant meaning.

A couple of years later, when I felt comfortable with my English skills, I enrolled in North Carolina State University. The University was kind enough to patch together all my disparate courses in Colombia into a custom-made curriculum that graduated me in less than two years with a degree majoring in business administration and communications.

On the family front, my aging parents found it difficult to deal with my little brother, and when he was about thirteen years old, they sort of threw him over the fence to us. I accepted this responsibility with no hesitation. We sent him to school, but he had many difficulties adapting to the U.S. culture. We sent him back to Colombia after a couple of years. This would be the first of two attempts to help him. But this experience helped me to understand more about what goes into helping others.

My husband's job with IBM routinely took him to many parts of the world, and I traveled with him as often as possible. Everywhere I went, I felt enriched, accumulating experiences and stretching my perceptions of people and the world. My eyes and my heart were open, and my thirst for knowledge was being satisfied in various ways. Unknowingly, I also was acquiring more practical and valuable life skills like flexibility and adaptability. And I finally became a U.S. citizen without losing my Colombian one. Those were violent years in Colombia, and the government there took the position of understanding why some might want to leave.

FOUR

The World of Doing

Inevitable globalization forces were imposing dramatic and rapid demographic changes, and relationships between people from the traditional and new cultures in the local communities were growing more strained every day. While I was fully engaged in my personal activities, my inner compass was paying attention to the social environment around me.

Living in the U.S. for a while, I knew that race issues are a way of life. For sure they had become part of my life, too, as I tried to figure out what being classified as a "person of color" meant. I had never heard this expression before. Who had no color? What was wrong with just classifying me by my name, Aura.

To me people were people. Growing up in Bogotá, the first time I saw an African American person was on a vacation trip to the Atlantic coast when I was maybe five or six years old and when my eyesight was so bad that I just saw shapes of people. Later on, when I was in my early teens, one of my parents' tenants was a single mother with a son. They were of African American descent. Still there was nothing different about them that I noticed, although I perceived something demeaning about how my parents, particularly my father, treated them. Then I forgot all about it. Later on, my encounter with the Native American people in Ecuador made me realize that they were also present back in Colombia, but that I hadn't noticed them and never heard anything about them.

Some say that one sees what one looks for, and the eyes of my soul only saw people—all kinds of people with varying percentages of Native, African, European, and Asian ethnicity. I only saw that there was so much in common. What was it that separated us so much?

From my own experience I knew that the lack of bilingual English/Spanish skills accounts for a lot of misunderstandings, and that it takes several years for a person to become proficient in a foreign language. What could I do to help a better understanding among all people?

The hands of Spirit were quite active behind my thought process, and soon I found myself in the local and new Latin American/Hispanic communities asking people to organize an artistic representation of all the ethnic groups in their country of origin. I was using what was closest to my heart—dance, music and visual arts—as the media to illustrate the racial and ethnic similarities I knew existed throughout the Americas: North, Central and South America. My parents had been great dancers, and their love for music and dance that they instilled in me became a crucial instrument to connect people from diverse cultures throughout my later fieldwork in education.

I invited several dance groups to form, including one from Colombia of which I was the organizer as well as a dancer. We all got busy with each group choreographing, rehearsing, and making costumes. When all was ready, I began taking the groups wherever I found an opportunity to perform.

A couple of years went by, and one day I received an invitation to bring a Latin American ensemble to perform in the International Festival that still takes place annually in Raleigh, North Carolina. This was the first year that the festival had a Latin American component. I was ecstatic! Furthermore, my heart was delighted when I heard that the theme of the festival that year was the Native American cultures of the United States. The festival also included performances of the European, African, and Asian American segments that make up the U.S. culture.

The day of the presentation, other members and I of the Colombian group were waiting near the main stage where we were to perform after one of the celebrated U.S. Native American groups. I was dressed in a costume for the first dance and was carrying bags and who knows what else in my hands—all the things that I would need to change into for our next performance. Then I heard someone shouting, "You can't perform. The schedule has changed. We don't have time for you to perform." "What?" I thought to myself, turning my head to see that these uncaring words were coming from the main stage coordinator. I then looked at the people she was shouting at, the Native American group. They looked hurt and resigned.

I was boiling inside, and my heart was in pain. Infuriated, I said to the woman, "How dare you! If anyone has the right to be on this stage it's them," pointing to the group of Native Americans. "They are the theme of this event!" I exclaimed! I was so angry and animatedly talking with my hands and whatever was in them—bags, shoes, clothes as this is sort of normal for me. Some of the Latin Americans thought I had gone nuts and that I was going to hit the woman. They ran away, looking for my husband to have him try to calm me down. The truth was I felt violated by the experience. The insult felt personal, and I had to do something to try to protect this vulnerable group. I encouraged them to go onto the stage to perform. They did, but only to hold hands for a minute or so in protest, and then left.

I didn't make the connection that this force had manifested before. It did, for example, when my father was threatening to kill my mom with a gun, in my interaction with the homeless children, at the bullfight, and around my sensitivities toward native people while living in Ecuador. It would take a long time for me to understand what was behind the force that propelled my heart to speak. This time though, it took over my experience of life. And it was so powerful that it forced me to surrender my mind and body to its will and take action.

The International Festival took place in late October, and by the following February, I was filing the incorporating papers for the Latin American Resource Center, LARC, a nonprofit agency dedicated to building bridges among people from all cultural backgrounds through arts education.

Above is the logo I created for my agency. It was to be the last painting I did for years. The journey afterwards would take my creative spirit into unknown places for a span of two decades. I became a cultural activist!

My husband fully supported my efforts including subsidizing the festivals out of our own funds for several years, and I found a small core of volunteers. For many years, the agency's office was in our home, and I didn't earn any income.

****

I was so inspired to give voice to the commonalities I knew existed among people from the Americas. Every time I thought about it, my heart sang and my desire to broadly cast the message grew stronger. Full of conviction, I moved to bring together the participation of Native, European, African, and Asian delegations from the U.S., and I requested each Latin American country delegation to bring theirs. The first LARC program at a Latin American Festival would be the first of its kind in this part of the U.S.

To my surprise, some of the Latin American/Hispanic participants thought their countries didn't have people of Native and African ancestry. Furthermore, for some there was hesitancy to share the stage with people of those ancestries from the U.S. It appeared that for them even considering the idea was repulsive!

Wow! I felt the impact of their strong reaction, and my curiosity was piqued. My thoughts ranged from how was it possible that people can feel and think this way to "Aha!" This was an essential aspect of the problem I was trying to understand. What could have been a deterrent went to fuel a stronger flame in my heart, with deep faith and trust, to pursue my work no matter what. My inner compass was taking me in the right direction.

The festival took place with great success and went on to become an annual event. My curiosity had found its reason, and my creative switch was fully turned on. Left behind were my own pains, like times when I was treated as an outsider when looking for a job in the Latin American/Hispanic communities of Chicago.

✳✳✳✳✳✳✳✳

To illustrate my vision of what the eyes of my soul saw that united the Americas, I researched the ethnic distribution of Latin American countries and the United States. I was intent on using the research as an instrument to give credence to what I saw was a most needed regional dialogue.

Gathering the data in itself was very telling. This was in the early 90s, and I found limited statistical data on ethnicity in Latin America. In some cases, like in Argentina and Mexico, there was no data about their African and Native populations.

I understood why some people reacted negatively to my requests. Wrongly, the narrative of their country of origin didn't include those groups, while it overemphasized the overwhelming influence of European colonization. I imagined that this probably was a major factor that kept me from seeing the Native Americans of Colombia.

The research showed that the same cultural groups exist in all the countries, although in different proportions reflecting on how they have been populated. For sure, in discussions of social issues, race in the U.S. seemed to be at the forefront, and this contrasted with my perception that in Latin America it was all about class.

On the surface, class seemed to divide people more in Latin America than race, and yet both African Americans and Native Americans live in higher concentrations on the lowest rung of the socioeconomic ladder. And whites, usually European

Americans, live in higher concentrations in the middle and upper socioeconomic classes.

This was also true in the U.S. Both regions had the same underlying racial and class issues. I realized that the difference is only in semantics. Categorizing people by race has been a major way society and life has been organized in the United States, while class has served that purpose in Latin America. But it's essentially the same thing.

I soon found myself in Colombia auditioning dance troupes to bring to our program in the United States. They would act as ambassadors of Colombia. I selected a group, and to celebrate, the Colombian President's Office of Foreign Affairs and LARC organized a public performance in Colombia. Naturally, I invited my parents to come, and it was clear that to my father, this was a bittersweet experience. I suppose he was happy and proud to see me in action doing my work, but at the same time he didn't quite know what to do with the presence of Native Americans and African Americans. But observing all this activity, he said to me, "You should have been an artist." I felt my heart stop. I reminded him of the tremendous beating he gave me for wanting to be one years earlier. I saw tears forming in his eyes.

✱✱✱✱✱✱✱✱

When I discovered that events like arts festivals are attended largely by those who already are sensitized to a larger world, I began outreaching into communities where these kinds of cultural enrichment activities are limited. My points of entry into the communities were local schools in rural and semirural areas.

Doing my heart's work wasn't easy, and yet there was a continuous flow of creative energy that moved me to realize my responsibilities. With no previous experience, I found myself totally immersed in lots of new activities like grant writing, fundraising, event production—and then promotion, public relations, hiring and firing personnel, budgeting, and public speaking as well as being a member of boards and commissions.

I was doing work that emanated from my heart. Two things were crystal clear about it. I had a conceptual framing —the commonality among people from the Americas—as well as the instructional means to realize it—the arts. The little voice inside me wasn't letting me forget my experience from the time when I couldn't communicate in English and began painting or as a child dancing and feeling like somebody. My work was informed by my own experience.

This clarity guided my work, which became an observational research project where one program led to the next and the next and so on. It usually began in collaboration with the central office for the county public schools by organizing a community working committee to create the schedule for the visit of an international dance and music troupe. I started with the country I knew best, Colombia. I facilitated preliminary teacher workshops and distributed instructional materials I was given by Colombian institutions. Teachers prepared multidisciplinary lesson plans. History, geography, reading, writing, math, languages, and sports were included.

A lot of effort on both ends went into obtaining travel documents. In one of the later programs, the group didn't get their visas processed in Colombia, and I was about to call the Office of the President when Senator Jesse Helms' office in DC made a call to the U.S. consulate in Bogotá, and at the mere mention of Helms' name, they got their visas and were on their way. At the time, Helms was a powerful conservative senator from my home state of North Carolina.

The troupe arrived for a week-long program. They visited hospitals, prisons, colleges, county fairs, and other places in the community. The troupe's thirty members were divided into small groups to offer workshops throughout the schools during the day and in community centers after hours. Adults and children choreographed a community performance that they shared with the one offered by the international troupe at the official closing of the program. This approach received the "NC Arts Best Arts in Education Program" award.

In one of their visits, I took a troupe to the high security federal prison in Butner, North Carolina. After spending hours getting through security where they scanned each and every instrument, person, and belongings, we participated in a most moving spectacle of human connection. The power of the arts melted down the physical, linguistic, and emotional barriers that separated the prisoners from the performing artists. Literally everyone present shed at least a few tears that day. Ah, the power of the arts!

It was fascinating for me to see the program impacting change everywhere in the most unorthodox ways. In a program that was taking place in Robeson County, I took the members of the troupe shopping. Everyone went their way selecting their items with no problem whatsoever. However, when they came to pay, they couldn't communicate with the cashier, and I was called to assist them. Only then were they perceived as different. Going by their looks, no one had noticed them. Robeson County is the home of a large tribe of Lumbee Indians and one of most diverse counties in the U.S. and the Colombian troupe members mirrored the very same ethnicities that exist there. They were all people with Native, African, Asian, and European looks.

Working with people in the schools, I saw the racial lines clearly defined in the way adults—that is, teachers, school administrators, and parents of different races and ethnicities—interacted and how their attitudes and behaviors bled over to the children. In my work with the schools, my eyes were opened to the pervasiveness and power of prejudice. One definition of this word prejudice is that it's the unfounded hatred, fear, or mistrust of a person or group, and distrust, a feeling that somebody or something is dishonest or unreliable.

On one occasion, for example, in the planning period for an international artist visit program, I noticed that at the school's headquarters, the offices were separated across racial lines. In a great divide, on one side were the offices of European Americans and on the other side those of African Americans. And I noticed that at our planning meetings, they barely interacted with one another and afterwards not at all. Then, as the program was implemented, the visiting artists, who themselves were by design a diverse group representing their Native American, European American, and African American Colombian roots, called my attention to the fact that at the program's final performance, a time for everyone to celebrate being together, students in the audience were divided across racial lines. And worse than that, African American students were sitting all the way in the back of the theater while the European Americans sat in front. "Why?" the Colombian artists asked me. In my heart I knew at least some of the reasons. My concern was what to do about this. What would help?

For a decade I had worked with adult participants, and I felt that I understood their issues. It was time now to know where children stood. The hands of Spirit guided me to develop and implement an international visual arts project as an instrument to find out what was in their minds.

I targeted middle school students in the United States, including new immigrant students and students in Colombia, asking them to draw their perceptions of people of Native, European, African, and Asian backgrounds in both the United States and Colombia. There were 3 different groups of children.

✳✳✳✳✳✳✳✳

1. LATIN AMERICAN CHILDREN LIVING IN U.S.

The following are examples of drawings by Latin American children living in the United States depicting their *perceptions* of people from different ethnic backgrounds around them.

The European American on the left has a whip in his hand beating an African American, who has fallen to the ground. A Latin American on the right looks on and laughs. (Stacey G., age 11)

A Native American in the country, cooking outdoors. The European American on the bottom is represented by the colonizing ships and being well received by the natives. (Maritza O., age 14)

An African American is outside his house, and above him there are images representative of the Ku Klux Klan. (Maritza O., age 14)

2. LATIN AMERICAN CHILDREN LIVING IN LATIN AMERICA

The following drawings by children living in Latin America represent their *perceptions* of Native, European, and African American backgrounds in the United States.

A cosmopolitan city, Hollywood, and across the river a Native American community. (Valentin C., age 14)

A day in the USA. An athletic African American with a boom box, in the middle a European American at his office, and at the bottom a Native American swimming. (Andrea M., age 13)

Above at top, a European American contemplates the Statue of Liberty that he holds in his hands. He is a scholar. In the middle, an African American man looks from behind bars with tears in his eyes from his cell. At the bottom is a colonial structure with a human image of a Native American peering through the front door. (Ivonne M., age 11)

✻✻✻✻✻✻✻✻

3. UNITED STATES CHILDREN LIVING IN U.S.

The following are drawings by children living in the United States represent their *perceptions* of Native, European, and African American people in Colombia.

A view of a Colombian countryside. There are two almost indistinguishable human figures on the right side. (Emlyn J., age 12)

An image of a soccer player with an inscription in English: "Do you remember the World Cup shoot out between Brazil vs. Italy in 1992? I do." (Chase L., age 11)

A man playing a guitar. (Michael C., age 12)

※※※※※※※※

With about 800 drawings collected we curated *Can We Move Beyond Stereotypes,* a traveling exhibit representing the major themes presented in the children's drawings. This exhibit was eventually donated to the Rosa Parks Museum in Birmingham, Alabama.

It wasn't difficult to realize that the children's drawings illustrated the dynamics I observed and personally experienced in the adult world. I understood that in different ways, their drawings told the story of what goes on in our society. Of particular interest was to notice that in the drawings from non-immigrant students from the United States, the students didn't see diverse racial groups existing in Latin America. They mainly saw poverty.

How much were their perceptions informed by direct experience and how much by the attitudes and the behavior of their role models at home, at school, and in the community? I decided that in the end, it didn't matter what the source was. What mattered was that these perceptions were in their minds. Thus, they were already limiting how the children saw their world and their lives.

In the debriefing sessions about their drawings, I heard the children speaking of a world that is plagued with prejudice and distrust. A world full of fear. I felt an arrow piercing my heart. In my mind I knew I was dealing with these issues, and yet there was something quite strange to hear the children expressing their beliefs and feelings. This intense experience caught me off guard.

The children's insight hit the nail on the head about what is at the heart of human suffering. My heart heard, "Fear is the root of prejudice and distrust. It causes pain in the heart." My mind heard, "Preconceived perceptions are endemic. They are passed down through generations" and the children of today are aware of it happening. Over the years, I had sensed this to be the case, but seeing it crystal clear like this, I became afraid of the truth.

My heart shuddered again when a similar exercise with adults produced images that conveyed stereotypes that were also clearly illustrated in the children's drawings. There was no doubt, and I repeat it again, preconceived perceptions are like the seeds of a genetically predisposed cancer that is ready to manifest any moment—particularly when feeling threatened.

I didn't know how big, how monumental this truth was, and how deep it would dig inside me. I didn't know at the time that Spirit was by my side illuminating my inquiry. Afraid of my own fear, all I could think and do was to find ways to allow others to come to see this situation with the eyes of their soul.

****

In the late 1980s I had begun my work taking performing groups, mine included, to perform for an hour or so. Now, a decade later the initiative involved county-wide and week-long academic and enrichment education activities that were reaching thousands of people in urban and rural areas in the U.S. and Latin America. I never thought to gain personal recognition through my work, but my heart was happy to receive accolades from President Bill Clinton and the National Association of Counties, NACO, who called it one of the best diversity initiatives in the United States.

I didn't see it then, but the program had become an itinerant educational laboratory. Something inside was telling me, though, that I was finding a way to educate in a new way in a rapidly changing world. And I began seeing a vision of something—a large and well-established educational institution perhaps, someday taking over the program to do it justice. My agency was not that, and nowhere in my heart had I intended otherwise. My inner compass was focused on something else of which I was not yet completely aware.

Meanwhile I became a community leader, a public figure, and a pioneer in the field of education. I was inducted into the North Carolina YWCA Academy of Women in the education category. Throughout the years I was a member of boards and commissions. Among them were the NC Closing the Achievement Gap Commission and the NC Human Relations Commission. I was inducted into leadership programs such as Leadership Triangle, Peter Drucker Fellow (Frances Hesselbain Fellows), William C. Friday Fellowship for Human Relations, and National Association of Arts Presenters. And all of my involvement informed me that prejudice and distrust showed their ugly faces in other societal ills like poverty and unequal justice.

I observed these kinds of problems creeping into the most unexpected places. One time while participating in the planning for the annual conference of the North Carolina Closing the Achievement Gap Commission, my ears hurt and my heart shuddered again when I heard a fellow commissioner, an African American, quite emphatically opposing the participation of an African American student as one to address the audience at the conference. She said, "These students—minority students—are not capable of doing a good job. They will embarrass the commission." Many others and I spoke against this statement—but she prevailed.

Prejudice, distrust, and fear were alive and living within this body charged with addressing the issues that were causing a 30% student and teacher dropout rate. No one seemed to notice what was happening, and a revolving door where attitudes and behaviors were perpetuated was well in place. Programs and policies kept on coming down the pipelines of the dysfunction created by prejudice, distrust, and fear. There were, I observed, constant wars between all the education stakeholders. Each group, including the students, at one point or another was declared the cause of the problems in education.

Thinking about these things may sound grandiose, but I felt the weight of this situation on my shoulders. I didn't realize that when my heart heard the children declaring *fear* as the culprit of human dysfunction, I felt fearful for the future of humanity. Fear was the root of human suffering. But checking inside me, I knew that I have felt fear, but I had no clue about what it was made of and, therefore, didn't know how to counteract it. I chose rather than confronting the unknown, to get immersed in a roaring sea of urgency. It was a powerful decision and moment in my life. It felt like a struggle to survive. It went above and beyond the passion and commitment I ever felt toward my work. What was the next step?

I felt blessed to find a new partnership for my programs. It was the school system of a semirural county in North Carolina that was experiencing great social and demographic changes. It was geographically divided between the haves and the have nots. It was a largely rural region relying on immigrant labor force that its traditional population was not ready to accept. David Duke from the Ku Klux Klan had been there recently, demonstrating on the main street. Furthermore, there was distrust between people from the community and those working for the public schools system.

As collaborators, we took each step of all that had worked well before in my agency's program, and over a three-year period, added the input given by the students, parents, and teachers. A lot of meaningful work was done.

I saw, for example, the shifting in the attitude and behavior of a school principal who at the beginning of our joined initiative, when discussing parent participation, plainly said to me, "those parents, what can they say of value?" He was referring to low income parents. By the second year I saw his eyes and those of his welcomed parents and children shining as they greeted one another. The program was growing strongly, and I could see that attitudinal and behavioral change can only happen through long-term initiatives.

An example of the change of attitude was when people who at the beginning wouldn't interact across racial lines came together and identified what they considered were the needs of their community. Based on their findings, they designed, created, and donated a mosaic to the county commissioners. The mosaic beautifully showed a community swimming pool, transportation connecting the extremes of their county, a health center, and a soccer field. Cooperation and hopefulness were in the air.

I remember one day when Madafo (a.k.a. Lloyd Wilson), a renowned visiting storyteller, sought me out in the hall on his way out of the building to say, "It is such a pleasure to participate in this program." And then, intensely looking me straight in the eye, he said, "You are a very thorough person." This was a rare moment. It was a moment that felt primal. It was like the person that he was talking about wasn't me. I had never considered myself thorough. But I always had been focused on doing any and everything possible to offer educational opportunities that were sensible and interconnected with the wants and desires of the participants. Indeed, preliminary sessions were solely dedicated to learning what children had on their minds for their summer program. I was always impressed with the quality and depth of the ideas that they provided.

The program became rich with learning opportunities. As a part of working with the *Can We Move Beyond Stereotypes* exhibit, I added identity workshops where participants began to share more of their personal stories. The identity workshops were a co-creation of LARC and the "Newspaper-in-Education (NIE) Program of the Herald-Sun," a newspaper in Durham, North Carolina. I was getting so close to something Spirit had been hinting at me for a while.

In my busyness when one initiative was coming to its final phase, I was already halfway into the next one, following an invisible thread sustained by a sort of magical force, of which I was an instrument, to do certain things.

I was on a mission, walking along a not-so-easy road. I was in a whirlwind, so focused on both present circumstances and quickly moving on to the next, that I wasn't taking the time to process all that was happening around me, good or bad. How did all these things figure in my own inner life?

My agency was a shoe-string operation with little operational funding, mostly made up with lots of personal sweat equity, which is not atypical in the nonprofit sector. Problems like meeting the agency's payroll responsibilities kept me up at night. There were times when I felt sad and angry about the actions of others directed at curtailing my work. It seemed that the more interesting and intense the program became, the more adversaries I found on the way, driven by, most likely, their own biases and fears and, possibly, professional jealousy and envy. On one occasion, doing the work of the state's Latin American/Hispanic Commission, there was time allocated in the agenda to hear about initiatives that were taking place in the state that related to our work. Several of the commission members had already presented their initiatives, and yet when I requested time to present mine, I was given the same story I knew so well that there was no time in the agenda. After all, my work was addressing some of the issues the Commission was working on, whether they were willing to admit it or not.

None of this stopped me, but, nevertheless, I felt treated unfairly. I couldn't ignore a certain understanding that some of these attitudes derive from a mentality of scarcity, when in my world there was enough for everybody. Nevertheless, I was getting really tired of the nonsense of the work politics. I took some solace from the times when my husband, my bedrock supporter, said to me, "You are not on the leading edge as some claimed. You are on the bleeding edge." He was right. It was a pain, and there I was figuring out how to move forward with my work.

In retrospect, the truth was that I had been running a laboratory that was searching for the answers to the problem of the fear that negatively affects human interaction and condition. Necessarily, this environment nurtured creativity, and there was innovation and excitement in the air. It also generated controversy because of all the negativity generated by fear.

"Where did the energy come to do the work?" I was asked one day by one of my critics. My answer was from my own intuition. He looked puzzled, but I was being truthful. Something was guiding me and I was having fun. I felt childlike delight in the same way I continue to have when, for example, I see birds coming to drink from or bathe in the water fountain I put out for them.

Around this time, I was thrilled to learn that the producers of "Models of Teaching," a UNC-TV program, wanted to feature our initiative in the partnership in the semirural community in their programming. I was really excited. This could be a determining factor to bring the program to the attention of those who could apply it to affect systemic change.

Nevertheless to my complete surprise, the school coordinator and my main contact severed what had been a positive relationship and our collaboration with the school system. I'll never really know what happened, but whatever it was, there was nothing that I, nor anyone else, including the NC State Superintendent for Public Schools who knew the initiative well, could do to avert the cancellation of the program. Just like that, the almost realized dream of a long-term collaboration with the schools went poof!

First, I was dumbfounded. Then I began getting angry, really angry at the World. And between my heightened sense of urgency and the impact of this shocking experience, something else happened. I began to see with the eyes of my soul the shallowness of so much of human activity that is dedicated to meeting the wants and desires of the ego. I was becoming disillusioned with this element in the human experience, my own included. I strongly felt its negative impact on me.

※ ※ ※ ※ ※ ※ ※ ※

Around the same time, the end of my role as a surrogate mother to my youngest brother was peaking. This was very significant in my life since I had always tried to be of service to him. I wanted him to heal from what I could imagine was a difficult childhood. Years had gone by when he couldn't adjust to life here, and one day he decided to go back to Colombia. I was learning that there is a time when it becomes essential to let go. I had to let go of whatever it was that made me think and feel I was powerful enough to change his life experience. When he decided to go back to Colombia, I experienced a form of death. I felt sad, but I put my pain behind the door in the usual way. I was too busy to take care of these things.

FIVE

Revelations

Lost, I continued to run my life as usual. But my life wasn't as usual. It was hard to define, but something was in the air that was affecting me in more than one way. What was it? An awareness began seeping through my existence announcing that I needed to let go of the busyness. But my mind resisted.

I gathered myself together, and for the next couple of years implemented several programs including a TV series where I had guests on to discuss issues like education and immigration. I also produced the news in Spanish in collaboration with WRAL-TV, a local NBC affiliate.

I was approached by the Democratic Party and took their challenge to run for an at-large seat on the Wake County Board of Commissioners. Still not giving up, I thought it could be a way for me to get to decision makers who could help bring LARC's educational program to the next level. And in doing so, Spirit persisted in exposing me to more of the human drama I was trying to change.

Campaigning in a small suburb north of Raleigh called Wake Forest, I got lost and politely asked a young man for directions. When he heard my foreign accent and that obviously I was campaigning, his face got red and full of hatred. He spit on the ground at my feet and left me standing speechless.

But positive experiences came my way as well. On the same campaign trail on another occasion, my husband and I attended a Sunday service at a rural church. We were the only non-African American people there. Unexpectedly, the minister took the time to acknowledge my presence and requested his audience to support my candidacy. He said, "If she has the guts to come here, she deserves our support." They even passed the hat and offered some money which, out of respect, I accepted. Dark and light sides of the human drama were before my eyes to see in a very personal way.

Running my campaign, I also learned about the huge role money plays in the political process, which I found very distasteful and unethical. Although I finished this first campaign with a healthy forty-seven percent of the vote, I decided not to continue down the path of politics.

I couldn't see at the time that the doors were opening for me to look in a different way into the fountain that fed my perspectives and my involvement with the World. Although these activities were important and time-consuming, Spirit was still offering me the choice to continue the exploration that fed my passion.

My uneasiness slowly became desperation, and my inner dialogue now took the form of me writing questions to Spirit. "Dear Spirit, why am I feeling so uncomfortable with myself? What is wrong with me? Where does this level of passion I feel toward my work come from?"

First Revelation

One night, I had the following visionary dream.

I was admiring the southwestern pot I acquired on my first trip to New Mexico. I was holding it in my hands. The pot began to spin slowly at first and then more and more rapidly. I was astounded. The spinning got to be so fast that because of its friction against the air, the pot exploded into a thousand pieces. Then I became the pot and began to spin. As I completed each turn, I saw a different human civilization in all of its splendor, and then its demise. Egyptian, Roman, and Greek temples, pyramids and the like I saw as magnificent structures and then as rubble.

At some point, I stopped spinning and began moving forward. I began to see a human figure sculpted onto a marble column. I was moving very quickly toward it. As I got closer, I saw that the figure was that of a woman. She was very beautiful with long white hair and was quite old. I began to fear that I was going to crash into the column and her. I began to see that she looked cold and stern. She was angry. She had a sculpted figure of a heart in her chest. I looked down at my left hand and saw that I was holding a heart in it. I was about to crash against the woman when I put the heart I had in my left hand over her heart. When I did this, the woman's face softened, a white light emanated all around her, and she said:

"All is well when the content of the heart is considered."

It was the most striking and divine moment of beauty I've ever experienced. It felt huge and all-encompassing. It was the wisdom of the times, eternal wisdom manifested. This was an incredible experience I trusted had really happened. I was mesmerized and felt blessed. The history of humanity, something that I never gave myself the time to consider, had unfolded before my disbelieving eyes. Where did all this information come from? Who was this ancient woman? Why was she so angry, stern, and cold? How was it possible that at the meeting of the heart in my hand with hers she transformed into a radiant and magnificent light?

This would be my first of several mystical experiences. But despite recognizing immediately that my dream was mythical and important to me in some as yet unfathomable way, my mind was still preoccupied with my conviction that my life's purpose was to deliver a humanized education methodology to change the ongoing human drama. My mind wasn't prepared to entertain any questioning about my doing. I felt lost.

Still, my mind kept on revisiting the majestic images of this first vision and asking questions about it. The hearts connecting felt nurturing, but whose hearts, were they? And again, who was the woman and why was she so angry? I loved the message at the end of the vision "All is well when the content of the heart is considered." But what did it really mean?

It should have been so easy for me to interconnect the visionary dream to the children's assessment about humanity's heart full of pain, feeling hurt by my recent frustrating work experience and the content of my heart. But I didn't. I couldn't get it.

Second Revelation

One night, exactly one year later, a thunderous masculine voice broke into the night, interrupting my sleep asking me:

> "How long are you willing to see things only half true and remain in darkness?"

That was it. Nothing visual, no story around it. Just a loud and commanding voice communicating something. Some call this experience a locution (paranormal), a mode of supernatural revelation.

I was by myself this time, as my husband was traveling overseas. I opened my eyes asking who are you? Why are you telling me this? Needless to say, I was perplexed by the words and authoritarian tone I heard. I knew that in no way did I possess enough power and clarity to come up with this kind of question. The spoken words were not of my mind and I was bewildered by them. This was more real than real. That was the end of my sleep that unforgettable night and for many nights afterwards.

I took the message personally. The darkness sounded somber and dark in a nasty way. Something of a devil's nature. I had to think again about my desire to do good in the world. What darkness was there in that? Was I a bad person and didn't know it? What did "seeing things only half true" mean?

****

After I gathered myself from the shock of the education program being canceled, I got busier than ever. I began to run my own community-based after school programs independently from the public schools. I was following my intuition telling me that the program had gone deep enough and was touching a primal chord about the human condition, and that it was necessary to continue looking for solutions.

I'd seen the perpetuating seeds of the human drama in all ages everywhere in society, and for sure, embedded in the education process. I also knew that to affect attitudinal and behavioral change, the challenge required a long-term approach.

I kept going around in circles in a sort of who comes first, the chicken or the egg kind of question, trying to figure out which age group was more at the heart of the problem than others in order to focus on the right group to drive an overall change.

I had worked with all age groups, and by now I understood that the learning process must be all about supporting the expression of the creative in each individual. I considered that endemic issues like growing teacher attrition and student dropout rates were more related to the education process and not so much with what was being taught. Overall, I understood that teachers were caught between meeting the constantly changing demands of a dehumanized education system and responding with their craft to the challenges they saw and experienced in the classroom.

I also knew that outside of the home, children spend most of their time with teachers. I decided that teachers were my program's target, and my creativity went to envision, create, and implement a two-year teacher apprenticeship program. I wrote grants, collected enough funds to run the pilot program, hired a couple of employees, and created a community committee to select the participant teachers.

My goal was to offer the teachers all the support possible. It was most essential to establish an emotional baseline by offering them quality time to express themselves and be heard, as well as to integrate into their teaching content and tools what they heard as requirements from the program's low-income families. The core of the program took place during the summer. I thought there was something of value to do more program follow up, so the program was designed to be sustained throughout the regular school year in an after-school fashion.

The initial group included a racially and gender-diverse group of five teachers and five college students. The teachers acted as facilitators and the college students as their assistants for three hundred students. Both groups were paid for their participation. The program took place in rented space from the local state university.

The first week of the five-week-long summer program was dedicated to participants sharing personal stories. And just as I had imagined, their stories acted as a mirror reflecting a vast spectrum of the human drama that adults and children carried in their heart. Even though I wasn't clear what it was, the hands of Spirit were guiding me to follow the thread that struck a chord within me early on when the children spoke about the pain in the heart.

One student, for example, shared about his life at home. Every day, very early in the morning, he fed breakfast to his younger siblings. Most of the time there was very little or no food for himself. He came to school hungry. A teacher shared about her frustration having to choose from teaching what she thought was relevant to her students and teaching to the test. A parent shared about the shame he felt being perceived as ignorant.

Based on the shared input from the first week of the program, the teachers designed a four-week-long integrated academic and enrichment curriculum. Students formulated a business plan to produce t-shirts with their own art. They looked at their own issues with education and researched how these issues played out in other parts of the world. They produced "The Invisible Child," a play about the real-life story of one of the immigrant students and his dilemma of feeling totally ignored in the classroom and the ways they thought teachers and parents could address this.

The school day started with a guided meditation for everyone in the program, and throughout all of the activities, students were learning, among other things, math, reading, writing, geography, history, and developing presentation skills. Teachers had a weekly session with a therapist and were offered a weekly massage. I was directly involved in managing and facilitating the identity workshops.

****

The first-year program evaluation reports were superb. Teachers talked about how much experiences in the program were positively affecting not only how they saw their students and others around them, but how they saw themselves. One teacher said, "Participating in this program is affecting my life above and beyond the classroom." That was it! This is what my heart was waiting to hear. This is what my soul was waiting to see. My heart reverberated to the point of almost exploding, hearing these kinds of testimonials. Here were the attitudinal and behavioral changes my soul knew were possible. Here was another affirmation of my perception. Attitudes and behavior change only from within. Here was an affirmation to what I had learned all these years. No policy and no amount of money or power could make this kind of change happen.

Here was a way to get to that sacred space in the human experience where each is able to begin to heal the heart and be moved to act out the creative flow of the force of life that runs within.

I began to imagine this happening everywhere. My thoughts went wild. "People need to know about this. How can I make this initiative go viral?"

And as all this excitement was being manifested, at the other end of my experience, I was dreading each moment of my life. I was burning the last bits of stamina left in me, arriving at total burn-out. But my mind acted as if nothing this merciless was happening. It was not as if I felt heroic, but like on other occasions, I was learning about the destructive power of mental habits through this miserable experience.

The administrative operation of my small agency had always been strained by the lack of proper funding for the scope of its programming, and now, since I no longer had the stamina, things got a lot worse. I continued to work 24/7 trying to figure out what to do to address the circumstances that were growing more complex in my work. But I quickly was running out of fuel while still focusing on my mission to deliver the best I could to help the World. Period.

In the second year of the teacher apprentice program, I added a new cohort of teachers to participate in a "train the trainer program." But my physical health finally took a drastic and dramatic turn. Psychosomatic symptoms manifested. I had a frozen shoulder. I couldn't sleep. I felt exhausted. It was hard to even open my eyes, not to mention getting up in the morning. My body began to scarcely show up every day for the program. I dreaded each moment, and yet my mind pushed me to keep working. John was constantly traveling with his work, and when he came home, usually on the weekends, we got busy handling some of the things he could help me with.

I was busting my brain trying to identify what was going with me and felt strangled by the self-imposed pressure to bring my educational program to affect systemic change in a broader sense. But I was depleted. My life had become painful and exhausting! It appeared as if my inner compass, my old friends' faith and trust and the hands of Spirit, all seemed to have disappeared. I wasn't looking into my own mirror.

My anxiety kept on growing. In desperation, my questions to Spirit got more emphatic. Somewhere within I found clarity to feel committed to whatever was unfolding on my path. My thirst for the truth was prevailing, and I got the courage to finally ask Spirit, "What is the need that I have to serve society, humanity? Where does this derive from? Is it a selfish driven need or is it a true calling? Please God, guiding light, Universal energy help me to see with clarity the real purpose of my life. Help me understand what is driving my behavior, my thinking, and my soul. Why can't I stop my work when it is killing me? Please tell me the truth no matter how painful."

I felt blessed to know that my good old friends' faith, trust, and the hands of Spirit hadn't really disappeared. I had just been ignoring them.

But within all the confusion and chaos, clarity also began to appear. The program was ready to be adopted by the educational department of one of the local universities. There was nothing else left for me to do with it. My thoughts were that institutions like this had all the resources to continue developing the initiative, while affecting change at the systemic level. I thought I could make this happen and desperately began implementing a public relations campaign, my third effort, directed at public officials in the legislature and the state's university system. Teachers, students, and parents shared their experiences of the program with them.

The habits of my mind were still functioning on high alert and trying to move me a little bit more, wanting to give more life to what I had been an instrument of Spirit to create. No one was listening. It all fell on deaf ears. When I heard the familiar words, "You are doing a great job. It's a great program. Just continue working with the teachers," I, for the first time, heard an inner clear voice saying, "That's it. I've had it. I am done!"

Such extremes of emotion were brutal. Increasingly, there was this sense that my life was being turned upside down and inside out. The upside-down phase was the chaos my body, mind, and work were experiencing while I was in the mode of "changing the world." The inside-out phase was the emotional bleeding I was experiencing and didn't want to acknowledge. Nothing else but changing the world mattered to me, and it was as if the train I was riding on either had no brakes, or I didn't know how to use them.

I remember a thought I had about the irony of the situation when at a board meeting, I overheard one of its members commenting about how much I was able to do with so few resources, and someone asking, "Could we clone her?" If only they knew how I was feeling, which they couldn't because I never talked about my own needs.

And in my soul's excitement and in the beating of my heart, I still couldn't hear or see how much it was shouting loud and clear for help. As always, I was not inclined to ask for help anyway and much less when it was about my inner workings.

This inclination had manifested clearly and was reinforced sometime earlier when I was going through a difficult time dealing with several situations. I was working a lot, my husband was often gone traveling for his job, and my little brother was experiencing some challenges. I was feeling lonely and out of sorts. My emotions were running high, and in one of my crying spells, I said to my husband, "Please I need help." I felt desperate.

Someone referred us to a mental health facility. Not knowing anything about the mental health system, I voluntarily committed myself. I did not know what to expect. I found myself in what, for all practical purposes, felt like a prison. Immediately after I came in, they brought me in into a teeny, tiny room that was stripped of any furniture except for a cot. The nurse gave me instructions to change into a gown, which I did, and she took my clothes, put them into a bag, and took them out of the room. Then she came back and put a tag on my wrist. I asked her what was going on. She told me, "Well, you have to stay here until a doctor comes to evaluate you." "What? When is the doctor coming?" I asked. "Well, we don't know for sure, but you will spend the night here," she answered. I continued, "But I came here just asking to talk to somebody." Coldly she repeated, "You have to wait until the doctor comes tomorrow," and as she was leaving the room, she made sure to close and lock the door. I was speechless. Needless to say, that was the most miserable night in my whole life. I had been institutionalized, and by my own hand. Just like that. Then I got angry, and stayed angry, fuming all night.

The next day, late in the morning, the doctor came and sat across from me looking suspiciously around him. I couldn't believe my eyes, this guy looked afraid of me. He said, "I am here to evaluate you. I understand that you are having some difficulties. Tell me, what is going on with you?" I said, "Sure. I am here because I am feeling overwhelmed, and I am crying a lot for no reason. I need help." "I see," he said. "So, are you depressed?" "Yes, I am." I answered. "Are you a threat to your life?" "No. And by the way, this is not the place I was looking for when I asked for help. I don't need to be held like a prisoner. I own my life." He asked again, "But you are depressed, aren't you?" I replied, "Yes, I *think* I'm depressed, and what is wrong with that? The whole world out there is full of depressed people. Are they all going to end up being institutionalized like this? I am acknowledging my emotions, and I need help, and this doesn't look like the place for it. I don't belong here." There was a pause, and then the doctor, with a barely noticeable smile of grace on his face, respectfully I felt, looked down and signed a release paper that he handed to me saying, "It was a pleasure meeting you, Ms. Maas." I just freed myself from hell, I thought. In the outcome of this wicked episode, I felt empowered and trusting in my capacity to figure out things for myself.

※※※※※※※※

Along with everything else weighing on my shoulders, and totally unacknowledged, menopause was hitting hard, messing with what I felt was my innermost being, the cell structure of my body. I was failing miserably to see that I was a workaholic, totally consumed by a great illusion. And my mind kept ignoring Spirit's call, the call to look within!

Meanwhile, in the midst of the turmoil, I also failed to notice that something was going woefully wrong at work, and I was rudely awakened when all hell broke loose. Teachers had grown deeply antagonistic and divided across racial lines. Given the first-year results, this should not have happened, and I was caught totally off guard.

Another dynamic had unfolded right in front of me. It began with my hiring an employee to write a grant proposal and help coordinate the program. When the proposal came to my desk it was as if it was written by someone that didn't have a clue of the program. I found myself rewriting the grant proposal against a last-minute deadline and driving close to midnight with it and my frozen shoulder to the post office and having a car accident—fortunately not a very serious one. It was a telling of my disastrous state of being. I had no energy. I was running on fumes. I was killing myself.

I fired the employee. She was very disgruntled, and before leaving our offices, she destroyed the agency's computer files. I went to the police's cybercrime security division, and they arrested her and charged her with a crime, for which there was a conviction.

One night during this episode, I became quite distraught when I was leaving the office because I wasn't able to move my car—someone had blocked its wheels with used tires. I thought that either this ex-employee or a friend of hers was in back of this. I became afraid for my life and stopped going to the office. My husband and I installed a security system at home, and I took a class in self-defense. This was the first time in my life that I actually felt fear for my life.

The now ex-employee went to one of my funding sources and accused my program of racism— this individual happened to be of African American descent from the U.S.—and me of misuse of funds. The funding agency proceeded not to reimburse my agency for our incurred program expenses, which made it very difficult to continue given our shoestring budget. People at the funding agency knew me and the integrity of my work, and still they blindsided me by the politics of race. I felt betrayed.

I canceled the two-year teacher apprenticeship program with a quarter to go, and this meant, for the first time in my life, I didn't live up to a commitment. True, no after-school program took place as planned, but still it didn't feel right not being able to pay the teachers their last payment. Much later I learned that the same ex-employee had caused the upheaval among the teachers in training by constantly pitting them against one another.

I went to Chicago to get away from everything, and while there, for no obvious reason, I tripped and fell flat on my face while walking. I was taken aback by this experience, which I took as Spirit telling me "live or choose a path toward sickness or death." I had a choice to continue what had become total chaos and kill myself or stop all of my doing. I chose life. This was the first time in my life when I actually became conscious of making a decision to stop my train of activity. Along with a frozen shoulder, a sort of inner paralysis had begun to take over my experience of the world.

This was a grim picture. Death was on the horizon.

SIX

The Dark Night of the Senses

My aging father got deathly ill, and I traveled to Bogotá to visit him. We had the best conversations ever. I shared with him about my troubles with the death of my agency. He listened intently, I thought. We didn't address anything about the past. We said our good-byes. When he transitioned three months later, I was awakened by a turmoil inside of mixed feelings. I felt relief, and I felt guilt about feeling relief. It was weird. On one hand, I felt relief from the fear and the distrust in my relationship with him and from keeping our boundaries in check all the time. I felt guilty thinking that feeling relief was almost sacrilegious, because he was my father. And at the same time, I felt tenderness toward him. The truth was that I perceived that he lived a tortured life that made him torture others around him. I felt that his life from very early on was full of uncertainty and pain, which by his actions he inflicted on those around him. Like my mother, he had tried to commit suicide. This happened, I was told, as a reaction to my mother leaving him in a rare move toward her independence.

But his presence and energy in my life had been monumental, and at its core, it took a lot to endure him. My mix of feelings felt so paradoxical. I can imagine that there must have been times when I felt angry at him, and that maybe the fear of his reactions was stronger. At any rate, I think my relief came from realizing that in our relationship, his suffering and mine were over.

Following my heart, I took a soulful opportunity to create a memorial service for him. In a small and intimate chapel in a convent, a beautiful chorus sang the Ave Maria, and my mom, a couple of brothers, and some close friends and I celebrated his humanity—both the good and the bad. I didn't know I had it in my heart, but I was able to sing a song that he liked. He was not a loving father, and yet in my spiritual memory of him, I was able to manifest the kind of feelings and environment I wished we had had in our lives together. I found my spiritual connection with him and love followed.

When I came home after burying my father, my agency's lawyer, who I had hired to process getting our final reimbursement from the government source, unexpectedly passed while at her desk. I was shocked. She was in the prime of her life.

✼✼✼✼✼✼✼✼

It had taken a long time to come to this point. What began as me feeling uncomfortable with myself and not being able to be fully present in my work, now was a complete paralysis. At the physical level, for all practical purposes, I disappeared from the external world, letting go of all that it had meant to me.

At the emotional level, all I was capable of doing was to sit in solitude day after day in the living room of our house, a room full of light and cheery enough to lose myself staring through the windows at my garden. My husband was gone most of the time with his work somewhere overseas. I didn't care that the minutes and hours were passing by. There within the emptiness I found inside, I cried and cried emotions that came from I know not where.

My pain was excruciating at times, and increasingly, I felt devastated and very tired. Months went by, and I began feeling dry inside like an old overused rag with all my tears spent. My heart ached, and I felt like I had no arms or legs. And then, in a quiet moment, I realized that my passion was gone. I cried to the heavens, where had it gone?

Feeling directionless, I found myself beginning to examine my life, something I hadn't done much of before. It began by looking at my work situation. I saw that I had been totally immersed with affairs of the external world, and that somewhere in the process, every step I took was a constant struggle. Somehow the dynamics of the work had changed from working for something to always fighting against something. This went against the grain of my natural inclination toward the positive and constructive.

It was sobering to realize that I had been repeating the pattern I had in my early life, always confronting my father's negativity. I had self-sabotaged myself. No wonder I became depleted and angry. But quietly, my old friends' faith and trust were whispering to me that in the larger sense, all was well.

At some point during this time, I had a first glance at me being the angry woman in my vision. I also had a feeling that there was something else that I needed to know about the woman in the vision, but I didn't know what it was… yet.

As I began to recognize and acknowledge long forgotten emotions, my mind opened up to consider other aspects of my experience. I felt blessed that I had the opportunity to totally dedicate myself to exploring my soul's desires. Nobody had forced me to do what I did or the way I did it. I felt gratitude toward my husband and his unconditional support. I felt gratitude toward friends and others for being there for me.

Although I had not officially closed my agency, I knew it was finished. I found great comfort in realizing that not only was I okay with that, but I also wasn't missing any aspect of it. It had taken some doing to finally stop the train I was riding on, and now that part of my life was over!

I felt deep satisfaction in knowing that I had found the universal truth *that fear is at the root of human suffering,* and my work had resulted in a method to grapple with it. I felt a sense of completion, and with it, I was able to acknowledge that my journey had been well-traveled and worth it. I was at peace with it. But in my newfound awareness, there were still moments when I felt overwhelming frustration and anger toward the world. I was learning that the world of emotions is both complex and confusing.

The world I lived in appeared so fake, and big words like leadership sounded empty. I thought more about it, and a couple of memories came back. I recalled an activity held in one of the leadership programs where I was a student. We were asked to "think about how you want to be remembered." I had difficulty in figuring out what to say even though some participants were quite emotional about it. The eyes of my soul saw that exercises like this reinforce the overidentification with ourselves and nurtures the perpetuation of attitudes and behaviors that further inflate our ego and help instill a calculating personality. "Was this the basis for the troubling distance between the head and the heart?" I asked myself.

The other memory was about a time when I was told by a progressive legislator, "Supporting your program would mean committing political suicide for me." In the context of the situation, I heard this person really saying, "I am afraid my constituents will not vote for me if they see I am supporting a Latin American agency." The logic of this escaped me. The program was addressing the needs of all people in this person's district. Where was the difference in our agendas?

Sometimes I felt like my mind was becoming quieter and quieter, and its thinking deeper and deeper. Thinking about the little voice inside, I knew hearing it was different from my earlier experiences of the visionary dream and the divine revelation command I received. I wondered whether Spirit and I were one and the same. At times I found myself in a place within where only perception existed devoid of my mind doing any qualifying, judging, or blaming.

And yet at other times, I felt at the opposite end, hanging from a thin cord that barely connected me with the World. I was swinging from one extreme to the other, between my mixed emotions, wrathful anger, despair, pain, relief, gratitude, and love.

Nobody could come to my rescue because I couldn't begin to describe what was going on within me. Plus, it was not like me to ask for help. This was one of my deep conditionings that I hadn't yet learned to let go of—giving myself permission to ask for help. So very much like when I lived through my family's drama and the abuse from my father, I lived through this situation without seeking to escape it or be rescued.

In the midst of it all, there was a surrendering, realizing that I, the warrior in me, couldn't force anyone to experience what my soul and heart were touching. I stopped feeling like I was in control of the external world.

****

There was the leftover legal issue of recovering the unreimbursed funds from the government agency after my lawyer's sudden death. I hired my dear friend Bill Martin, who had retired from politics, to follow up with this. He was a leader in the African American community, and I met him when he was a state legislator. We were both participating then in a town meeting in a rural county in North Carolina where my agency, in collaboration with the local school system, was implementing our educational initiatives. The meeting was attended by county commissioners and other public officials. After introducing ourselves, each offered some words. I said mine and then was quiet. The meeting continued, and at some point, the person next to me passed me a little folded paper. I opened and it read, "Aura, speak up. Bill Martin."

This was the beginning of a precious relationship. He was one of the kindest and wisest persons I was ever blessed to know. I saw him as the personification of integrity. He was a lawyer and a one-of-a-kind state legislator who only cared about doing the right and moral thing. He cared about people, regardless of their racial and ethnic roots or influence. And he tirelessly worked on behalf of everyone.

He had retired from his legislative work, and one day he came to visit. Angels must have been with us as we had a soulful conversation. We reminisced about the work that bridged our connection, and how important it was to each of us. I shared with him that I was at peace closing my agency, and that I didn't miss any of that world. I also shared with him that I was clear that if I lived again under the same circumstances, I would do exactly the same about everything in my life. In other words, I had no regrets. His last words to me were, "Thank you. I feel at peace around you." This was to be our last visit. Death continued to be a theme in my life.

He left, and I went back to my oil painting, an early interest I was rediscovering in my new life. I knew he hadn't been feeling well, and from time to time I thought about him. A couple of times I said to myself, "I am going to call him." One day we got a morning call from Pat, his wife, to tell us that he had died. I was beyond sad. Even today I sometimes want to hear his voice and his words of wisdom.

He passed right before taking action on my agency's behalf to recover the unreimbursed funds. I finally took all of the recent deaths in my life seriously. I decided that it all indicated that the time had come to finish once and for all the business of my agency.

As a final act, I hired an auditor who produced a report refuting the accusation of misappropriation of funds, and I sent it to the government agency that had withheld my funds. I never heard from them, and I did not pursue this any further. That was the end of that. I closed my agency after twenty years of its existence. I was letting go of the warrior stance that had become one of my personality's signatures. This is the way of Spirit.

****

In the past the affairs of the external world had been my focus, but now I was beginning to feel inspired and illuminated by Spirit to give in to my curiosity about the state of my inner self. Something inside me was changing, and I continued to surrender and give myself over to more looking inside.

Coming out of my self-imposed exile, I joined the world again by taking a required study program to become a Reiki practitioner, a Japanese healing technique that is administered without touching the body to channel energy in someone. It is based on the idea that an unseen "life force energy" flows through us and is what causes us to be alive. When the flow is blocked, problems arise and Reiki aims to correct this. The idea of exploring energy now strongly appeared on my horizon, this time with the intention of using it as a healing technique.

The theme of energy mattered to me. It had been since the time at the farm when I saw the fantastic number of ants moving harmoniously in unison in one direction only. I felt they were propelled by the force of life. I thought our lives must also be impacted by it. How could they not be?

Since I was a child observing my father's predisposition toward the negative and how it influenced outcomes with people and situations, and thinking there must be an opposite force, a positive side, I often wondered how things could have changed for him and all of our family if he could have balanced the two.

I was delighted when I realized that to be a good energy worker, I first had to make clear to myself that I was in a good space myself. This was powerful learning and new doors were opening. Before offering a Reiki session, I sat quietly in meditation clearing my own inner space and energetic field. As I started the work, I lit a candle as I felt myself and the other person in the presence of Spirit. I had known about Spirit intuitively, but now I could feel it and be more present and available in ways I hadn't experienced before. Helping others had always been on my radar, and now I rejoiced at the idea of being an instrument of Spirit to channel the life force for healing purposes.

Guided by Spirit, I was experiencing a major transition. I was moving from the paradigm of "doing" to the paradigm of "being," and learning and applying Reiki was perfect in that it demanded of me to just *be!* Plus, the hands of Spirit were assisting me to learn more about breaking down the energy blockages generated when fear overcomes our experiences.

****

The book, *The Four Agreements* by Don Miguel Ruiz, was given to me by my dearest friend, an angel. Its wisdom strongly resonated with me. It says, "Putting out love and gratitude perpetuates the same in the universe" and "be impeccable with your word and that will reflect in your life and your relationships with others. This agreement can help change thousands of other agreements, especially ones that create fear instead of love."

His words resonated with me. The idea of putting out love and gratitude and changing agreements that create fear instead of love applied so much to the direction my soul had taken me.

In my earlier life in Colombia, I intuitively managed not to internalize my father's long-lasting discord and anger and my mother's submissiveness and victimhood. And all of my work on education had been about devising a method to change agreements manifested in our attitudes and behaviors. And the force behind all of it was my soul's desire for harmony and independence, both an expression of love.

This kind of grappling was so refreshing. Honestly, I never really spent much time thinking about things like where my focus and my creative energy came from. All I knew was that I was on a mission to address my concern about humanity. But new doors of understanding were opening for me, and I encountered a most interesting situation when I, for the first time since I stopped my work, ventured out seeking further understandings.

In preparation to go with John on one of his business trips, I researched things to do while he was at work. I found and immediately signed up to participate in a workshop Don

Miguel Ruiz was offering. The event was taking place at the Pyramids of Teotihuacan near Mexico City, a site that was a religious center and was home to over 100,000 people at its peak in 450 CE.

I joined a group of about twenty people to participate in the magic of the life process through the honoring of our ancestors. After introducing ourselves, we walked throughout the pyramids in meditation. I particularly remember one moment when we were taken into a dark cave, a place we were told usually is not open to visitors. The deeper we went into complete darkness, the more I felt a growing sense of comfort. Something in me wanted to go deeper, be there, stay there. I have never experienced this kind of reassurance in dark places before.

When we walked out, we were told to pick up some stones and to hold them as we thought about what was in our heart and what brought us to this journey. This was a walking meditation through the sacred valley between the Pyramids of the Sun and the Moon. (These pyramids built by the Aztecs were used in unknown religious ceremonies.)

I wanted clarity about the meanings of the visionary dream and the auditory revelation. I wanted to know what was next on my path. Whatever it was, I was ready for it. After an hour or so, we were to meet on top of one of the lower structures.

I did my walk and headed toward the meeting point. When I reached a flat area, I saw one of Don Miguel's assistants coming in my direction. When we met face to face, I felt her body begin melting onto mine without touching me. It was really quite eerie. I reacted by crying, and she hugged me murmuring in my ear "Remember, I came to you only because you are ready." It was a powerful and confusing experience.

I left the workshop before its end due to a previous commitment I had with my husband in Mexico City. So, I didn't have the chance to inquire about what she meant by me "being ready." Ready for what? I knew her body was melting onto mine. It was as if the field of energy that was her enfolded mine, and I became afraid of what that meant for me.

I was taken aback by this experience. I felt the power of the encounter between energy—the melting of her body—and fear—the overwhelming emotion it provoked in me. I was caught in the crux of the short circuit their encounter caused.

I left the place knowing that I had experienced something more real than real. I knew the experience had happened, and yet I couldn't explain it logically. I left the place knowing that life and the human experience are multidimensional. I was between bewildered and excited in the company of my old friends, faith and trust.

I also left the place with the sculpture shown in the photo. It depicts a snake, a jaguar, and a condor, which now I know represents the Incan Trinity. In Inca cosmology the condor represents the upper world, the world of spirit. The jaguar represents the middle world, our everyday plane of existence. The serpent symbolizes the lower world, the depths, the subconscious. The sculpture is a symbol for all three worlds.

The snake is one of the oldest and most widespread mythological symbols that have always been associated with some of the oldest rituals known to mankind. Historically, snakes represent fertility or a creative life force. As snakes shed their skins, they are symbols of rebirth, transformation, immortality, and healing. Intuitively, I always have been attracted to snakes. These symbols would appear again in my experience.

I had entered a magical world, and my perspectives of objective reality were expanding. I was placing myself within the flow of the divine creativity that was already unfolding.

This perspective was a hell of a lot better than the previous one that had me passionately working myself to death to do my soul's work to "change the world." I was full of gratitude for this realization. I should have felt a great relief except that the power of the mind and its habits really hadn't given up totally yet.

※※※※※※※※

I was exploring where my new path was taking me, and all my mind could see was a blank in front of my eyes. This was all new to me. As far as I could remember, I had always intuitively known what my next step would be and would positively move in that direction. Now I felt lost and beyond disconcerted. My heart was in pain. And I grew impatient. In spirit I felt ready for whatever was next, but didn't know what it would be. So, I felt stuck.

Meanwhile, after my father's passing, I had become my mother's caretaker over the Internet, by phone, and visiting her in Colombia occasionally. On one of my trips to see her after my father's passing, I took her and her best friend, an angel, on a road trip to the Zona Cafetera in Colombia where prized coffee is grown. We were in a hot springs resort, and I offered my mom a Reiki session in a quiet corner. Two gentlemen came by commenting about their familiarity with the practice. We engaged in conversation, and before they departed, they suggested that I read some of the works of a modern philosopher by the name of Ken Wilber.

When I came home, I followed up and learned that he is a prolific American writer on transpersonal psychology and integral theory. It seemed to me to be in line with a teacher I had studied in the past, Sri Aurobindo, an early 20th century Indian philosopher and poet. Now I felt affirmed to find someone contemporary giving me the same sentiments. To survive my early years and then to affect change in the world, or what I call "the world of doing," I realized that I had actively been working as if I were following Wilber's theory that expounds on a system for the synthesis of all human knowledge and experience.

In studying his work, I saw reflected in it the unfolding of my life and consciousness. Based on Wilber's system, instinctively I had moved from what he calls the Consciousness of my initial experience to activating new Behaviors such as changing my eating habits and stopping the perpetuation of the behaviors of my parents, then to Culture by founding an agency to affect change in the world, and finally to Systems by addressing a systemic process to affect that change.

I began feeling like a bulging flower bulb ready to spring back into life. I felt like I was pregnant and ready to give birth to something. It was an uncomfortable feeling that made me anxious. What was it? I thought that perhaps sharing my findings about education and the teacher apprenticeship model that derived from it was my next step. I began writing. I also put together the workshop, *When Thinking becomes a Servant Awareness: A Conversation from the Heart.* One of the participants from a leadership class I presented it to said, "the workshop was a personal testimonial of holistic leadership. Head, heart, and stomach—failures, success, and unknowing— were brought together from her personal account."

I still had a desire to further my education. I was moved to apply for a Master of Arts in Liberal Studies program at Duke University. But I was told by a man, a member of the advisory committee and the one who denied me entrance to the program, that "I didn't have the intellectual curiosity to accomplish the program." This went against what the woman director of the program thought who saw that my participation would be a great asset to the program because of my extensive field experience. I thought the man was crazy, and I let it be only one more interesting, frustrating, and telling experience around the field of education.

✳✳✳✳✳✳✳✳

Over a long weekend, my husband and I were hiking in the North Carolina mountains and there were many families around. We were on a difficult trail recently opened to the public, and some of the caution signs were still missing. We passed by a large family with small children. Later on, we heard an unusual sound and thought it probably was an animal rushing through the bushes. Then we heard someone screaming. We ran toward where the sound was coming from to realize that a four-year-old child had gotten loose from his mother's hands and slipped under the split rail fence guarding the trail, falling down a cliff. He was killed.

The family spoke only Spanish, and I was able to help them communicate with the park rangers and thereafter with the state authorities. This was a horrific incident that brutally showed me life's fragility once again. Death showed its face again. I fell deeper into the void.

By then I was doing lots of physical therapy to heal my frozen shoulder, and following my intuition, I also gave in into seeking help once again. Following the little voice inside that was telling me that my vision and revelation had elements of universal patterns and images, I chose an archetypal psychotherapy treatment.

This effort didn't go well… again! After some sessions, I found the therapist looking like she was falling asleep as I was telling my tale. I found this to be true when at the next session, she started talking about something I had never told her. Whatever it was didn't really matter, but I was sure she wasn't really hearing me. Or maybe she just couldn't understand me. After all we had different accents. That was it for me!

****

A few months later, when close friends and I were sitting in their living room in Chicago, a friend called to let us know that a Native American medicine man (a healer or shaman) was visiting town. He was going to do a healing ceremony on the evening of the following day. I felt my being go on full alert. I looked at one of my friends, who is psychologist and a serious spiritual seeker, and enthusiastically said, "Let's do it!"

The next day we interviewed the medicine man over the phone, and we committed to participate in this ceremony that would use a Native American hallucinogen. I called my husband, who was traveling on a business trip, and told him about my plans. His immediate response was: "Let me sit before I fall down." He was absolutely stunned by my news. I had always been militantly against the use of any consciousness altering substances. He asked me, "Have you gone crazy?" "No," I responded. I was centered and present in a way I never felt before. Even though I wasn't clear about what the intake of a hallucinogen meant, I wasn't apprehensive at all! I spent the whole next day fasting, meditating, and taking a cleansing bath in preparation for something that felt very sacred.

There were about ten participants. In the introduction I learned that the name of the medicine we were about to take was San Pedro, a cactus, and that it is a member of the mescaline family. Shamans and natives have used it for at least 3,000 years. The name San Pedro came from a myth about God hiding the keys to heaven in a secret place, and the Christian Saint who was named San Pedro using the powers of a cactus to uncover the secret hiding place of the keys. Later the cactus was named after him. I also found out from the medicine man that San Pedro is energetically a masculine plant. I didn't know there was a gender quality to the plant kingdom! This was news to me.

At the ceremony there was an altar at the center of the room. It was dedicated to the Virgin of Guadalupe, the patron saint of Mexico. The medicine man offered a prayer, and the ceremony began as each participant took the first dose of the plant potion. It was a thick, slimy, and acrid liquid served by the medicine man to each of the participants. It was served in a small cup, and each of us was given a small bucket to put by our side in case we needed to vomit. I was given my potion and went to sit down at my spot. I held the cup while I mentally asked Spirit to give clarity about my path. When I felt ready, I held my breath, the way I learned to do as a child when taking a medicine, and I drank it. It wasn't a pleasant sensation, but I took it well. I didn't need the bucket like some of the others did.

Some time passed, and I didn't feel any effect. Then I asked for a second dose, and soon thereafter, I began a journey that ended eight hours later. During it, I became part of the life making process and, indeed, the beginning of life. It went like this:

> Suddenly I was in another dimension; I was not me. In recurrent cycles I became one with air, one with water, one with the Earth, and one with fire, as each in all-encompassing waves showed their full power. Each wave moved as though it had a consciousness of its own, and my con-

sciousness and its consciousness were *one* consciousness. At one moment it/I/we became a torrent of wind blowing hard that stirred up monumental waves of water as we drowned ourselves and the earth. Before we could recover, all became fire that consumed everything in existence, as visceral pain throbbed throughout my body evoking tears that felt ancient and primordial. They emerged both from my womb and from the center of Mother Earth's womb, and they transformed into laughter that soon changed to sublime elation and joy. Everything folded and unfolded to eventually merge into a celestial bliss, embedded in a divine energy and angelic music. The recurrent waves and cycles kept on feeding into one another, as did my emotions.

The only word I can find that may describe the pain and sorrow that I felt is FEAR, and the one that best describes the state of celestial bliss, where everything is in alignment, is LOVE. Fear constantly tried to take control with my uncertainty of not knowing what was coming next. I was afraid of disappearing, as feeling the particles of each of the elements stripped away all that didn't belong in my heart. Could I sustain the next wave? But I always did.

My fear was fear of not having any control of the situation. And yet all these tides of primal experience eventually passed, and LOVE emerged with a realization of completeness. In love ALL was well, and I was at peace. By the end of this journey, I came to fully grasp that fear is destructive and love is life-giving. But they are the two extremes of the same energy spectrum, like two sides of the same coin.

Toward the end, after eight hours on this journey, I became me again in consciousness, and I found myself in front of the altar of the Virgin of Guadalupe, totally suspended within another dimension of life where I was one with a spiritual essence. My physical body seemed to be contorted into some sort of yogic position I didn't know existed. But despite its strangeness, I felt the complete peace of being one with the universe.

All of a sudden, I heard the voice of the medicine man saying, "Wake up!" I came back to the here and now. And it happened just like that! And I wondered if my cosmic laughter and crying—they must have been obnoxious—had bothered others in the group. My brain still wonders about this. We all went to sleep, and after resting for some hours, we had breakfast where I shared my experience with the medicine man, and he said, "With that kind of experience, that is all the medicine you need to do." I was certainly puzzled.

Afterwards, we went home, and I invited my friend to go out for a walk. He agreed with some reluctance since his knee was bothering him. We went out, both quiet and lost in our thoughts, but he soon decided to go back home.

I felt vibrant and at peace walking on this beautiful early winter day. But my vigorous walk began to slow down as I began to feel my body getting heavier and heavier. I was not sure what was going on, but every step was becoming more and more difficult. There were no other symptoms. I was perfectly awake, breathing the freshest air ever and seeing other walkers pass by. But as my body slowed, it reached a point when I could not move any longer. I couldn't move even an eyelash, finger, or toe. Mentally I was fine, but my body couldn't move, and I just stood erect, keenly aware of my environment. The air was light and the breeze soothing. The daylight was crystalline. The birds were singing their hearts out, and the squirrels jumping from tree to tree. People looked happy walking their dogs. Some of them passed by me and looked at me, I imagine probably wondering what was going on with me. But no one asked any questions. I am glad because no one, not even I, knew what was happening. I stood there for what seemed like hours until little by little, I began taking small steps back home. What usually was a half hour walk took me about three hours.

I had become acquainted with a sacred space within myself that I didn't know existed. Right then and there, I also knew that nobody and nothing could ever touch it or violate it for the rest of my life.

SEVEN

Shamanism

In 2009, scientific and technological advances, all of which I recognize as manifestations of the creative life force, made it possible for me to acquire perfect 20/20 vision without glasses via cataract surgery! For me this was nothing less than a miracle.

But in the meanwhile, I was stuck between the interests of my mind and those of my soul. I was frustrated that my writing efforts were going nowhere. Surely, I felt I could use some assistance with it, so when I heard about an Integral Incubator writing workshop based on Ken Wilber's work, I immediately signed up. I thought that there I would get the proper support to write my book. Little did I know Spirit had something quite different lined up for me and that, given the kind of stubborn individual I can sometimes be, I would only learn about it the hard way.

I went to Boulder, Colorado to attend the workshop. John had arranged for me to visit Rocky Mountain National Park the day before the workshop was to begin. It was late fall, and there was already ice on the ground. As I stepped onto an icy patch to take a photo, I slipped. While trying to save my camera, I fell, this time not on my face, but on my precious right hand, the one that I write with. I wound up with a broken wrist and a cast. I debated about whether to stay or not. I decided to stay, and my husband immediately came to assist me, as I couldn't shower or dress myself.

It turned out that the workshop was not about writing a book. Instead, I listened to the many different ways each participant was seeking to impact the world. In a final exercise involving the delivery of an elevator speech on behalf of one's project, I felt that I miserably failed as a thousand words came out, all at the same time. I felt overwhelmed. Something was out of alignment. A small group had a session with Wilber, and I felt a kinship with him and his work, although it felt a bit too intellectual and unbalanced toward the masculine. But I had a sense that we all consist of both masculine and feminine energies, and our work is to bring them into alignment.

****

Later that year my husband retired from his work as an Internet software specialist with IBM in the U.S. IBM Brazil immediately hired him because of his many years working with them, and we went to live in Sao Paulo. I liked the idea and it felt like a great opportunity to expand my horizons in a new culture and country similar in size to the United

States. I had been there before and felt that the region was going through a time of hope with lots of creative energy. I wanted to be a part of it.

I found many similarities between Colombia and Brazil. One of them was their languages, Spanish and Portuguese. They are both romance languages that share so many similar words, but occasionally with differences that easily can get one in trouble. On one occasion, for example, a friend invited us for dinner, and I expressed my appreciation to the cook saying "Muito obrigada. O jantar foi exquisito," "exquisito" in Spanish meaning what it sounds like in English as well. "Thank you so much. Dinner was exquisite." I noticed that the woman's face got red and angry. Well, in Portuguese "exquisito" means "weird." I'd insulted her. Fortunately, it all became clear soon, and we all laughed about it. Moments like this are precious as I feel that they are an opportunity for the mind to become a little more flexible each time they happen.

But while I was adjusting to a new culture, my frustration about getting clear about my next step kept growing, and a year after moving to Brazil, I desperately wanted to know where I was headed. I couldn't see that since their occurrences, I hadn't stop grappling with the content of my mystical experiences. I was immensely anxious as I felt that in my writing, I was going around in endless circles. It was almost funny that I named a program I was writing about… Circles, An Educational Program of Innovation and Learning™.

This is what I wrote. "CIRCLES™ is an educational process that engages the minds and the hearts of students, teachers, and others in the community in sharing their knowledge and wisdom as they create a relevant learning experience, classroom tools, and instruments."

I didn't understand it at the time, but the lessons from my mystical and shamanic experiences were guiding the Circles process, addressing working with the content of the heart by acknowledging and honoring the interconnectedness of the human experience.

I failed to notice that the circle is a universal symbol that represents the notions of totality, wholeness, original perfection, the Self, the infinite, eternity, timelessness, all cyclic movement, and God. It is weird how the power of the habits of the mind can make things like this happen. These principles were already embedded in what I was writing about, but I couldn't yet see their relevance, and I was growing more and more impatient! Spirit hadn't abandoned me. I hadn't abandoned myself. It was my mind not wanting to let go, not trusting that life is a process, an interconnected process, and that my work was continuing. I had faith and trust that clarity was to come someday, but my mind wanted it now. That was my problem.

****

One day, my husband and I were again visiting our friends in Chicago. As it happened, the shaman I had met two years earlier was in town again. He was offering another ceremony, which I eagerly joined. In the introduction he explained that this time the medicine plant we would ingest was ayahuasca, a vine that grows in the Amazon. I was expecting the use of the same medicine as before, and for a moment I doubted if I should participate. But then he explained that this plant medicine works with the feminine energies. When I heard the word "feminine," my whole body went on alert, readying itself for the new experience, acknowledging intuitively that the theme of the masculine and the feminine had been lurking about me for a while.

I took the medicine, and this time all that unfolded was visual. I began seeing the vine of ayahuasca constantly moving, gently sliding, swirling up and down and around, and entangling and disentangling from all that she found on her way, just as a snake does. Wherever she went and whatever she touched, she left a trail of energy changing in shape, color, and direction, like a kaleidoscope. Millions of multicolored patterns moved up, down, and all around into infinity. It had a merciful and profound effect on me. It was harmonious, and I felt soothed and at peace.

During the ceremony, a strong and tall man was standing by the fireplace near where I was sitting on the floor. Later in the night, I heard a huge thud that made me conscious of the room again. When I opened my eyes, I saw the man lying on the floor. He had flopped down onto the floor. The shaman, with the help of others carried him to another room where he was taken care of. Thankfully, nothing serious happened to him. Later the shaman told us, "The medicine gives you what you bring to it." My understanding about this was that life, and perhaps the hallucinogenic experience, is a mirror reflecting our inner state. Maybe this man brought some apprehension, some kind of fear into his experience. I remained alert.

****

Shortly afterwards in Brazil, while visiting the coastal area between Sao Paulo and Rio de Janeiro, I encountered a spot where a river met the ocean. Suddenly, a metaphor unfolded, and the eyes of my soul saw our human lives as a river that eventually joined the ocean of our collective self, uniting as one. I saw the river as the masculine force and the ocean as the feminine, and I realized that, like fear and love, one can't exist without the other.

In the months afterwards, however, I grew more uncomfortable with myself, impatient and frustrated. I kept thinking about participating in an upcoming two-year shamanic study immersion program the shaman announced the last time I saw him. It sounded interesting. I was curious and thought that maybe I would get some answers there. I had been conversing with my husband about it, trying to decide whether or not I wanted to sign up. I would have to periodically travel to wherever each session of the program was to take place, for example, the Peru Amazon, the Andes, and New Mexico. I had no problem with that, and I knew my husband wouldn't either. I wasn't even worried about the cost of it, although the little voice inside was telling me that it would be good to pay for it with money resulting from my own sweat. At the time I wasn't making any money.

My real concern was about whether or not I should trust and give myself openly to this process. Was it the right moment, with the right people? I wanted to feel certain I was taking the right step. I was cautious. Spirit came along just in time and helped me make a decision in a most unconventional way.

My husband and I were in Chicago on yet another visit. He spent a week downtown attending a work seminar, while I was in the suburbs with our friends. I went downtown on Thursday to meet him and spend the evening together. Sometime in the middle of the afternoon the next day, we were coming back to the suburbs to spend the weekend. It was a Friday afternoon, and we took the L, or elevated rapid transit. It wasn't very busy that day and as we were nearing our destination, which also happened to be the last station, we got up, grabbed our luggage and prepared to exit.

As we readied to leave, I saw an older woman coming down the aisle. She and her hat and clothes looked quite strange to me. Everything about her was odd and strangely out of place. She looked emaciated, somewhat like a skeleton. I noticed she had an intense look in her eyes. I thought my crystal necklace had caught her attention. As she approached, she said to me, "Ah, that piece around your neck is from the Southwest." We engaged in a short chit-chat while the train was beginning to slow. I asked her what she did and she responded, "I am sick."

Then she corrected herself by saying she should not say that anymore. "My medicine man just told me I am healed." My husband John was listening, and at that point he interrupted, asking her who her medicine man was. He was curious given our recent conversations about my signing up for the immersion program. She said he was from New Mexico. Well, my medicine man (shaman) was also from New Mexico. Then really puzzled and excited, my husband asked her if she cared to share this person's name. We both couldn't believe it when she mentioned the name very familiar to us. She was talking about the same medicine man, my medicine man!

By then the train was already stopped, and the three of us began to get out with a few other people. Now I was really interested in continuing our conversation with this woman, but she seemed reluctant. My husband took off down the platform to give us privacy. As she and I walked together, we passed a small plant island in the center of the narrow platform. She went to the left and I to the right. At the end of the short island, no more than a couple of feet, and hoping to continue our conversation, I looked for her. But she was nowhere to be found! I was dumbfounded. She had completely disappeared. I reached my husband and asked him if he saw her pass by him. "Nope," he said. He then went ahead searching for her among the very few people in this small and scantily populated station. But she was nowhere to be found. She had vanished.

We were speechless. We went home, and in the evening, I finally said to my husband, "Honey that woman…" and he said, "Yeah, she was a ghost." That was exactly what I was thinking. This was quite telling about both of us. I instinctively considered all possible kinds of phenomena before I make up my mind. My husband, though, tends to be quite skeptical of the spiritual world. But here we were, declaring our experience in similar terms. We both saw a ghost. I remembered her legs dangling like two sticks. Her wrinkled hat, her craggy clothes, everything about this character was odd, as if from another time. My husband looked at me and said, "I guess that is a cue that you must sign up for the program." I did.

Later, I told the shaman the story. He said there was no such woman. He didn't have a client that met my description of her. He said to me, "You created her."

"What?" I said.

"You created her because it was essential for you that your husband actively participate in the work that you are doing, not as a result of being supportive of your efforts, but rather of being convinced by and from his direct objective experience." I listened in disbelief, I might add. But to this day my husband and I know that on July 24, 2010, we saw a ghost, a Spirit sent to help me along my way. There is no other way for us to describe what happened that day.

We remembered that we had had a sort of similar, but funnier experience back in the 80s when we, and another couple, traveled around Ireland. We kept hearing stories about the importance of respecting all the stones that had spiritual significance. One day we found ourselves visiting the Blarney Castle, which is a medieval stronghold in Blarney, near Cork. At the top of the castle lies the famous Stone of Eloquence, better known as the Blarney Stone. According to legend, the stone has the power of spirit to give anyone who kisses it the 'gift of gab' (or the ability to be a smooth talker). Who wouldn't want that?

So, we all were quite excited to kiss the stone and proceeded to do so. To kiss it, one has to lean backwards, holding on to an iron railing, being held by a guide, from the parapet walk. When our male friend's turn came up, he decided to be funny. He took a sanitary wipe out of his pocket and cleaned the stone before kissing it. The guide who was assisting clearly didn't think this was funny. You could tell by his facial expression and body language.

After our visit to the castle, we went back to our bed and breakfast with the idea of taking it easy before dinner. We were all resting when a scream interrupted the silence. Immediately we got up and headed in the direction where the sound had come from. There we found our friend who had wiped the Blarney stone, bleeding from his forehead. What happened? He said that in the room's darkness that he had gotten up from bed to go to the bathroom, and on the way, he hit his head against a wall.

Naturally, we were quite shocked. His wife proceeded to apply a butterfly bandage to stop the bleeding on his forehead. It wasn't helping, so my husband rushed him to the nearest clinic where he had the wound stitched. After a couple of hours, we all finally went to bed.

The next morning, we all went to breakfast and were quite chatty. Needless to say, we all had in our mind the experience of the night before and went about trying to describe what had happened. Our host was a wonderful lady to whom my husband related the story about what our friend did at the Blarney Stone, adding jokingly that because he "messed" with the stone's spirit, a leprechaun probably pushed him into the wall. She replied "Oh no, the wee folk didn't push him into the wall. They moved the wall for messing with the stone!" She seemed quite serious, and I felt the experience to be real.

Experiences like this bring back memories of the earliest time when the idea of the Spirit world presented itself on my horizon. We often laugh about this story, and some might call what happened there a mere coincidence. But to the owner of the B&B we stayed in, she spoke as if her conclusion was fact to her and her Irish community.

❋❋❋❋❋❋❋❋

Over the next two years the shamanic studies program took me to the southwestern United States, the Peruvian Amazon and its Shipibo-Conibo people, and to the peaks of the Peruvian Andean mountains and the Q'ero people. The Shipibo-Conibo are an indigenous people along the Ucayali River in the Amazon rainforest in Peru. The Q'ero are a Quechua-speaking community and ethnic group dwelling in the province of Paucartambo, in the Cusco Region of Peru. I joined with others in learning from these indigenous cultures. We camped, hiked, meditated, and participated in Despacho rituals designed to align, balance, and harmonize the three levels of consciousness: *Yankay* (the physical universe), *Yachay* (the spirit or wisdom center), and *Munay* (the feeling or heart center). In all that we did, we were learning to thank Mother Earth and the spiritual world for allowing us to be there and for providing for our nurture. Beautiful altars were arranged with flowers, grains, *agua florida* (a popular cologne used in ceremonies by shamans), and tobacco offerings.

In the information package sent out prior to the first session of the program in December, there was a request to bring our favorite healing pieces. When I read the request, a force took over my mind, and I said to myself "I must bring my turquoise necklace," without really knowing why. I was referring to the necklace I acquired on my first trip to New Mexico in the early 80s. With no hesitation whatsoever to pick it up, I traveled all the way from Brazil to my home in North Carolina where it was stored before going to the northern mountains of New Mexico where we were meeting.

I found myself at the first session of the shaman training in a rounded ceremonial structure called a maloca. It had a mesa, an altar, in the center where the other participants and I were asked to put our healing objects. I laid down my turquoise necklace.

Before the ceremony we took a walk, thanking mother earth and asking the four directions to guide the work that we were about to do. After doing this, we went to the maloca. When the ceremony was about to start, I felt compelled to get up, go to the altar, pick up my necklace and put it on. The ceremony started, and we took some medicine.

Sometime later, I began feeling overwhelmed with bouts of uncontrollable laughter. I knew I was disturbing others, but I couldn't control myself. An assistant came to help me quiet down. The force that made me laugh was so overpowering that I began feeling miserable and embarrassed.

Suddenly, the necklace began twisting and tightening around my neck like a snake, and I was having difficulty breathing. I felt terrified. In desperation, I called for help, and a medicine woman came and instructed me to take the necklace off. I did, and all my symptoms stopped right then and there.

She took the necklace and put it on the altar. Sometime later she came by my side and quietly asked me if I was familiar with the story of *The Lord of the Rings* and what happened as Frodo bore the ring. It was sucking away his life. I said, "yes." She told me that something similar was happening with the necklace. It had special powers. I listened. I was at peace as the ceremony continued.

Later, the shaman came to talk with me. He told me that he had to do a lot of work to negotiate being able to connect with the source of Spirit that could tell us about the necklace. He said that when he did, he was told that the necklace had ancient encoded information that had to do with humanity. "It is an oracle." He said it had passed through the hands of many healers throughout time who, unsuccessfully, had tried to decode this information. I listened carefully and then asked, "What is my role in all of this?" He said, "For now, you are the necklace's caretaker." I asked, "Why was it choking me?" He said, "The time to decode the information has not arrived yet." I asked who was to decode the information. He said it needed to be a very advanced medicine person. I asked if he could do it, and he said, "I wouldn't touch it."

He advised me to wear the necklace in ceremonies because he had seen its beneficial effects in elevating the vibrations of healing energy for everyone in the maloca. I walked out into the world knowing that something very profound and meaningful happened to me that night. I knew what I knew, and I didn't give in to my mind not wanting to believe what my senses had felt. I already knew something about these things from my previous experiences. Something inside me was singing, full of excitement and curiosity beyond words. I wondered what else was going to unfold.

****

Later, on my first trip to the Amazon, I felt drawn to the painting below by a local healer and artist.

It represents a worldview where a shaman is one with the forces of nature. When I saw it, I couldn't help but to feel a familiarity with it and a sense of empowerment. The force of life, my intuition, and Spirit were all beginning to manifest themselves to me through the lenses of the knowledge and wisdom embedded in the traditions of ancient people. I was very comfortable with these feelings.

The artist Pasquel Florez Agustin, who painted the picture, shared the story of Meraya, *The Power of Animals,* behind his artwork as follows:

> One day, Ronon Nico, a young man, began to do *dietas* of several medicinal plants, each diet lasting a year. He started to dream about many plants and animals, those you see in the picture. He grew older and got married. When he went out fishing, he came back with lots of fish and other animals like jaguars, parrots, snakes, alligators, and owls. He conversed with all of them, and sometimes he shape-shifted, becoming one of them. He then would disappear and then reappear somewhere else, becoming a Meraya, which meant that he could cure the sick with *mapacho* (tobacco) and *agua florida.*

"*Remember that you are WATER. Cry. Cleanse. Flow. Let Go.*
Remember that you are FIRE. Burn. Tame. Adapt. Ignite.
Remember that you are AIR. Observe. Breathe. Focus. Decide.
Remember that you are EARTH. Ground. Give. Build. Heal.
Remember that you are SPIRIT. Connect. Listen. Know. Be Still."

—attributed to Stephanie Mill

---

ns
EIGHT

The Dark Night of Spirit

John and I continued living in Sao Paulo. While he was working, I stayed most of the time in our apartment. We lived in a small, delightful flat, and I found myself getting into a daily routine, continuing being the hermit I was at home in the U.S., walking, meditating, practicing Reiki with a few friends, painting, and eating on a regular schedule. There was no anticipation about anything, and I felt more present and centered. It was as if I was just witnessing being and developing new habits.

Still, from time to time, my mind wondered as to what application this new state of being had for me. At a seminar and in my shamanic studies, I asked renowned spiritual leaders questions like "What am I supposed to do with the inner peace that fills my heart in a human world that I perceive so full of pain?" A couple of times I was told, "Never underestimate the power of such bliss. It can illuminate the world even from the darkest of caves."

Thinking back to when I walked into the cave at Teotihuacan, I felt that the deeper I went into the earth, the more comfortable I was. Not knowing why, I wanted to remain there. Something was calling me there. I had secluded myself in my home in Raleigh, and to a great degree, I was still secluded, for sure from the public life I lived before. Was this the cave they were referring to? And if so, how did it all connect to making a difference in the world? I needed someone to help me understand these things. I was really puzzled.

But I had no personal guru to go to. And I've often wondered about this. Where was my spiritual teacher? I never really had one, but it seemed it was a common experience for others. Was I missing something?

On one of my trips to the Peruvian jungle from Sao Paulo, our study regimen was to fast while doing a tobacco diet. A tobacco diet is an ancient practice to receive blessings and protection and to release toxins, anxiety, and other undesirable elements from the body. This meant that for five days, we spent the day drinking a flavorless tea made from dry tobacco leaves and resting in silence, except at dinner time. Each participant had their own hammock for meditation. I also walked outside around the maloca, contemplated the plants, listened to the symphony of birds and insects singing, and felt the harmony between the elements of air, water, fire, and earth. I made my own offerings, spreading tobacco around to Spirit and the elements, thanking them for all their blessings.

I was immersed in the beauty and bounty of the jungle, and I listened to the inner voice telling me about the mysteries of nature. One day I saw in a flash that the teacher I had been missing all my life, the guru that I had been recently asking for, was inside me. It always had been there. Oh my God! Lost in the cave of the womb of Mother Earth in the Amazon and in the darkness of my inner cave and womb, I recognized that a guru—God or Spirit—resided within all of us! All my life, I had had an intuitive relationship with something that felt sacred that I couldn't explain, but always wanting to connect with it. It was right inside me. I felt so quietly rich.

With this knowing and understanding, there came an awareness to humbly accept the seed of divine wisdom that is embedded in my human experience, and to realize that my guru had always been there in the company of my old friends, faith and trust and the hands of Spirit. This was what felt sacred. Now it was all clear. All is sacred and divine and resides within.

It was crystal clear as the purest water. My life was endowed with ancestral material to learn about the human experience, and I'd been learning to acknowledge and honor Spirit as the force of life. This realization was a defining spiritual moment and a most humbling experience for me. I'd found inside the space that I couldn't find going to church—nature was my inspiration.

In my mind and heart, I understood that I am an instrument of the force of life, and so is everyone else and all that surrounds our human experience. I saw that we inform one another's evolutionary process.

I felt comfort in realizing that the guru inside had always been there, synthesizing my knowledge and experiences into insights that deepened my understanding of relationships and the meaning of life. I felt stronger. Plus, I felt a profound peace in knowing that everyone and everything is a continuation of this eternal experience. This was such a beautiful and powerful realization, and yet the unfolding of the spiritual path is not linear the way the mind wants it to be. More reckoning with the power of the mind would be coming despite my insights.

* * * * * * * * *

Returning to Sao Paulo, I unexpectedly received an email from an old friend. I hadn't been in contact with this person for a long while. We knew each other from the time when I was doing my work in education.

She was heading a department of education at a college in the U.S., and after reading the initial salutation, my eyes got transfixed on the following words, "How would you like to head our Center for Excellence in Urban Teaching as visiting Director?" "What? Oh, my God," I thought, "this can't be true." I read it again and again. My eyes were glued to the words "Excellence in Urban Teaching," and my heart wanted to jump out of my chest. Was this the opportunity I so feverishly sought out earlier to expand my education programs through a university? My mind flew back in time, and I saw people of all ages and walks of life—students, parents, and school administrators—all closely working with teachers, learning from one another, and creating relevant education tools and instruments. I saw my dream realized. I thought, "she knows my work, so this must be it." I rejoiced.

I discussed her offer with my husband, and we considered several scenarios, including that if everything went well, the position could become permanent, and eventually, we could move to that area of the country. This is how exciting the idea was to both of us.

I got on a plane from Sao Paulo to my home in the U.S. to pick up some of my belongings, and then back to the world I had left several years earlier—the world of doing.

On day one, when she picked me up at the airport, and on our way to the office, my friend said, "You must know you are *not* to trust anybody on your team." My intellectual curiosity and my desire to affect change got the best of me. I didn't really hear what her words were really saying about the state of things at her work and what she wanted of me.

She didn't tell me she was at war with her staff, and that she was really looking for an ally. I'd walked into an impossible and chaotic working environment. A whole new experience had broken into my world of being. I guess Spirit had more lessons in store for me that I needed to learn about the difference between the worlds of doing and being. Uncharacteristically, I had let my guard down.

My hard work began. I quickly discerned that the drama in the situation wasn't any of my making, and it became clear that even though I cared, my loyalty to our relationship didn't mean I had to conspire with my friend's conflicted relationships. I was there out of my own volition and inspired by a constructive thought that I was keen on following. My attitudes and behavior toward my team members were not compromised, although I became one more of my friend's enemies. It was an awkward position, but I was okay with it.

Sadly, there was nothing new about the dysfunction that I had witnessed so often in my earlier work. The anger, distrust, and fear that the children mentioned were right there in the realm of higher education.

As in similar situations before in my life, I chose to stay the course of the experience, but in a somewhat different stance. My strategy was, regardless of the negative circumstances, to focus on actively exploring implementation of my program in that community. I shared with my team about it, and we rolled up our sleeves and developed a work plan. At one point, I presented it to the Center's Advisory Council, and even my friend commented on how good it was, not that it made any difference. Relationships were strained beyond repair, and my project was already doomed. It was just a matter of how long it would take for the ship to sink. My now ex-friend left her post first, and then the others and I followed. I went back to Sao Paulo.

Throughout my life, I had followed my inner compass, and this was also the case in this situation. But here I experienced a sense of clarity of mind that soon became my ally, and I chose my options rather easily without the usual pain and anxiety. This was a huge step forward for me. I felt my mind and heart uniting at ease. My tendencies had always been to go with the positive, but now I was acknowledging and honoring this approach not out of a survival mode, but consciously being present, fully alive, and responsible. This generated more space within me to feel compassion.

With the eyes of my soul, once and for all, I saw that the idea I'd been attached to for so long about the institutionalization of my program wasn't in my hands. Any leftover of that bubble in my thinking and in my heart was blown away. Spirit was kindly reminding me that I learn through my own experience through the eyes of my soul. Now I could let go of a frustrated idea my mind was quietly carrying inside.

Ironically, the desire I felt earlier about paying with my own sweat for the shamanic study program was realized with the money I earned in this job. The experience had been well worth it, and I was full of gratitude. Thank you Spirit! I saw an application of what I had heard before that spiritually one does not get what the mind wants, but what the soul needs for its own evolution.

✽✽✽✽✽✽✽✽

On another trip to Peru, while learning from the Q'ero people in the high Andes during one of the shamanic study sessions, I did a program solo night—a time to spend alone in the mountains away from the group to deepen and awaken my connection to nature, the spirits of the land, and the ancient ones. The idea of carrying all my camping equipment in a backpack to a remote location was quite amusing to me. Thirty years earlier, when my future husband asked me to carry a small day pack on one of our excursions to a rural area in Ecuador, I refused. I was a city girl who certainly would not act like a donkey trudging along with a load on my back. His request was mortifying, and almost ended our relationship. Who would want a husband who thinks of his wife as an ass!

Well, here I was with a full-sized backpack in Peru, in the Huayllay National Sanctuary, Bosque de Piedra or Stone Forest, at an altitude of about 4,500 meters (over 14,000 feet) trekking about like a donkey until I found an appealing site to pitch my tent. I put my gear down, assembled my tent, and went out to enjoy the area. I came back later as night was falling, and as I was getting ready to go to bed, I realized that I had lost my emergency blanket. I knew it was important to have it to add to the warmth of my summer-weight sleeping bag since the previous nights had been bitterly cold, enough to freeze the water in my water bottle. (Average daily temperatures there are between 18- and 59-degrees Fahrenheit.) But there was nothing I could do about it since night was falling, and I could not return to the group in the darkness of the very rocky terrain.

It began to get colder and colder, and my legs began to freeze as my body shivered. To warm up, I began meditating and doing visualizations, sending energy throughout my body down to my legs. But it was to no avail. I couldn't feel my legs, which meant I was losing control of them. I knew this to be a symptom of hypothermia since I suffered a bad case some years earlier while swimming in the never very warm Lake Michigan. I considered my options and felt there was nothing I could do. I couldn't move. And even if I could have, in the dark of the night, I didn't know which direction to take back to the base camp in the immensity of this national park.

I thought that that might be it for me, that I was going to freeze to death. I began to pray, saying thanks for my life and goodbyes to my mother, my husband, and others in my life. Then, suddenly an owl came right next to my tent. It started hooting, and I became mesmerized by the sound and fell asleep. When I awakened, it was morning, and the sun warmed my tent. I was fine. I had survived. I was full of gratitude toward Spirit and the owl. They saved my life!

Afterwards I remembered the little owl shown below that my mother gave me a long, long time ago. I somehow must have communicated to her my liking of these creatures. I felt gratitude toward her and the owl for being so attuned with me. It didn't dawn on me then that the owl was also present in the painting I acquired in my previous trip to the Amazon.

This is an entry in my journal about my experiences in the shamanic study program. "Working with native shamans in the jungle and Andean mountains has been a most profound experience. Now I know that understanding the truth about my relationship with myself, others, and nature is my goal. I ask of Spirit to illuminate me, give me clarity, power, and inspiration. I honor and appreciate the medicine people and all who served as instruments for me to come to this understanding. I have a deeper sense of peace and comfort."

NINE

The World of Being

John finally retired again from his work with IBM, and we returned to our home in North Carolina where I got as busy as a bee putting together my website, **innovatingforeducation.com**. On it, I wrote:

> The challenge facing all of us, individually and collectively, adults and children, rich and poor, people of all skin colors, and everyone everywhere is to take the first step toward acknowledging that our heart is in pain before we point the finger at one another. Throughout the centuries, we all have allowed dehumanization, and now it must end. Looking deep within our hearts, we must facilitate listening and dialoguing with others and, especially, our children. To be more exact, this must be the heart of the education process. We know it, and we can make it happen!

I was heartened to read a recent article in the *Los Angeles Times*, where the Dalai Lama said much the same thing:

> *"The time has come to understand that we are the same human beings on this planet. Whether we want to or not, we must coexist. My wish is that, one day, formal education will pay attention to the education of the heart, teaching love, compassion, justice, forgiveness, mindfulness, tolerance, and peace... We need a worldwide initiative for educating heart and mind in this modern age."*

Words were pouring straight from my heart. I was expressing what my soul eternally knew, but I was still caught in paying too much attention to the constant noise of the mind that is there from the moment of waking up in the morning to the moment of falling asleep at night, and that had characterized my world of doing. I hadn't figured out the meaning and application of my mystical and shamanic experiences, nor did I know the purpose of my life. I felt stuck, and I felt anxious.

Almost immediately after coming back to our home, we purchased camping equipment and began traveling to the national parks to realize a dream we had while watching a Ken Burns documentary series, *The National Parks: America's Best Idea*. From that moment to this, we have visited all but one of the parks in the lower forty-eight states, forty-seven of them out of the sixty-one in total. A new chapter in my life was beginning. My little inner voice was guiding me to follow another path toward quieting the noise of my mind.

On our first road trip to the West, while attending a powwow (a gathering of Native People) in Montana, we met a Native American man who engaged us in conversation. He asked, "Where do you come from?" I said, "from North Carolina." He looked at me intently and said, "Just remember. We are here to collect memories" and then left. My heart heard him saying that we are here to collect memories of our ancient past, ancestral memories. I thought about my parents, the grandparents that I barely knew, and their predecessors. How am I to learn about them when everyone is gone? I felt deeply curious and excited!

On a trip while visiting La Push, Washington, which is in the Quileute Indian Reservation on the Olympic Peninsula, I felt honored when I was offered a symbolic eagle feather by another Native American man. I felt honored because the eagle is highly respected in many world traditions, and because for Native Americans, it symbolizes great courage, strength, vision, skills, and a reminder of a person's connection to God. My own experience of the importance of our relationship with animals had begun intuitively a long time ago when I first purchased a snake ring that is always with me. Later I acquired the sculpture depicting the eagle, the jaguar, and the snake. The jaguar became the animal spirit guiding my shamanic study group.

In keeping with shamanistic thought, animal spirits choose us. It would take a long time for me to realize that, mystically, the three animal guides, the snake, the jaguar, and the eagle, that are represented in the sculpture of the Incan Trinity I spoke about earlier, had all appeared before me in a tangible way.

When the man at the powwow mentioned collecting memories, I was capable only of conceiving the idea that he was referring to blood ancestors. But in visiting Lake Louise in the Canadian Rockies, nature communicated something that blew my mind. I read a sign that said, "The water you drink here may have quenched the thirst of a dinosaur… or have been served to a princess!" Oh my God, this is an ancestral memory. This was what the man at the powwow talked about. The water in the lakes, oceans, rivers, frozen glaciers, clouds, plants, and rocks is the same water that has forever existed on the planet! And it is the same water that sustains our bodies, other animals, and all forms of organic life. Our tears of sadness and joy are made of the same water! We are made of the same water. If only water could speak!

This was a monumental truth manifesting so clearly and simply.

And whereas some years earlier, I felt at peace observing nature through the window of my living room, now I was experiencing it while actively hiking up and down the mountains, strolling around valleys, streams, and rivers, and following the sun, the moon, and the stars. My body was heavily sweating and my mind growing in expansiveness, while my heart calibrated all that was happening. All of this was happening in unison. My heart and the heart of air, fire, earth, and water were all one, while the eyes of my soul saw, crystal clear, the intrinsic interconnectedness of all that is. Nature contains all that is. Nature is sacred. Everything is a mix of the four elements. Life is sacred. Humanity is sacred. Nature is the temple I began searching for when I stopped going to church.

As time passed, my sense of reverence toward life and nature grew larger, the constant mind chatter—that I call the noise of the senses—was diminishing, and the inner empty space was occupied by a full presence and awareness.

And Spirit whispered more real than real events and visions. Perception was king, and the eyes of my soul were its instrument. At Yellowstone National Park, they saw the life-making process right before my eyes as Mother Earth spat out the ingredients that make the soup of life that is embedded in our nature. Every visit to a national park would be an opportunity to collect ancestral memories, and that I would be aided throughout with visions and spiritual gifts.

At Custer State Park in the Badlands of South Dakota, I began hearing owls far in the distance as we bed down for the night in our tent. My husband quickly went into a deep sleep while I kept paying attention to the owls. Images came to me of the owl my mother gave me a long time ago, the one that saved my life in the peaks of the Peruvian Andes and the one that appeared in the set of spirit animals that are shown in the shaman painting that adorns my altar. Their calls continued throughout the night, each time coming closer and closer to our campsite. Finally, toward dawn, a very loud call announced an owl next to our tent. It was so loud that it awakened my husband.

Before we bedded down for the night, I had given thanks to Spirit and all the elements for allowing us to be there before we set up our tent. I interpreted this experience as the owl blessing us back. I felt blessed as the owl as a spirit animal offers the guidance necessary to deeply explore the unknown and the magic of life and is emblematic of a deep connection with wisdom and intuitive knowledge. I also welcomed the perspective that says that the owl guides us to see the true reality, beyond illusion and deceit. I thanked Spirit as I continued to be committed to find the truth.

****

In this stage of pure perception, it seemed that there was nothing for my mind to construct or deconstruct, and yet something very profound in my experience was transforming.

The comfort, nourishment, and power of nature had been at my door since I was young. Now its basic principles were entering my consciousness and shattering basic and solid concepts my mind treasured. I began asking myself if there was any difference between the "I" (identity), and the "Other" (duality) when we all shared the same basic natural elements—water, air, fire, and earth—and have done this since the beginning.

Paradoxically, the sense of my identity and that of otherness began disintegrating. Big, old, very old, and great illusions began losing their ground in my consciousness.

I was a humanist and had always cared and respected every individual from all walks of life. I found similarities in behaviors and attitudes that had served as stepping stones for a lot of my involvement with the external world. I had detected the energy that seemed to move the millions of ants that covered our home when I lived on the farm with my parents. Yet, never before had I gone so far as to contemplate how much we humans share even in our physical bodies.

I felt elated grappling with these thoughts. In the world of doing human activity, observing behaviors and attitudes had served as my field of study. Now a new portal opened for me through direct experience, to observe and learn about nature's properties, its dynamics, and its interrelatedness to the human experience.

I discovered that the study of nature is the mine the human mind explores. And that in doing so, the mind exercises and expands its capacities to acquire, process, and replicate nature's ways. All scientific and technological knowledge emanates from there.

Meanwhile, as the eyes of my soul perceived the natural world, my mind and the wants and desires of my senses were growing quieter and more tamed. Nature continued speaking more clearly and loudly. An insect, a bird, a four-legged friend, a rock, a cloud, the flames of fire, or the roaring sounds of the winds blowing and water rushing through the glacial mountains were all elements of an intelligence. I understood that the force that I felt moved the millions of ants through our dwelling when I lived on the farm with my parents was also an expression of the same intelligence. I was now living in the world of being and it belonged to the spirit world.

****

Nevertheless, the realization of my life being the manifestation of life's eternal process, of which the "I" in me was only an instrument, was tested when in a casual conversation a friend said to me, "You are nobody now." He was referring to the leadership position I left when I closed my agency. My ego wanted to be offended by his comment. But with the passage of time, when I heard what he said with my soul, I realized that my friend was right in his assertion. In the linear experience of the world, I, by choice, was nobody. I realized that I could have decided just as well to pursue many other opportunities, and that I made the right decision following the hands of Spirit—my intuition and heart's desire. In my heart I thank him for making me realize the truth. I failed to see that this new consciousness was a direct answer to the curiosity about the identity of the "I" and the "other." These concepts were melting together.

Conversing with other friends about identity issues later on, I shared about my experience of being told that I was "nobody." I said that it felt right that I didn't have an identity, and that my next business card would say so, "Aura Camacho-Maas, Nobody." We were laughing about it when I got a phone call from Colombia about my mother's declining health. My husband and I immediately flew there.

I had my most heartwarming moment with my mother ever when she was in the hospital. I shared with her a funny situation that involved my husband shopping in Bogotá. We were looking for a pair of cosmetic support underwear a girlfriend had requested. It's slang name in Colombia is "levantaculos," or "lift your asshole," naturally something not said in public. My husband, not realizing this, used the slang word with the salesperson. When she heard his request, she burst out laughing, especially hearing the word with his English accent. Of course, she knew what he meant! My mother on hearing this thought that was hilarious. She and I became one with the experience and were lost looking into each other's eyes communicating the vibrancy of LOVE. This to me was the most intimate and sacred moment ever with my mom. Can't you imagine Spirit laughing about this? But as good an experience as it was, unfortunately this was the limit to our conversation. As usual she didn't have anything to say about my childhood or anyone in our family, including the death of my father.

In my last visit to my mom at the hospital, I used the bathroom. After I washed my hands, I looked up at the mirror to find that there was no glass mirror, only a frame. There was no mirror, and there was no image of me. I kept looking at it until I broke out in an uncontrollable, deep-down laugh that felt as if it was coming from the womb of the earth. There it was. I, literally, was "nobody." This felt refreshing and liberating as if more of the weight I carried on my shoulders was lifted off. And I realized that a lot of the drama that characterized my life was gone, and that that space within was occupied by a sense of expanding peace and joy.

My mom passed on a short time after I left Colombia. I was sad that I couldn't be present when it happened. I would have loved to have been by her bedside, letting her know that I loved her. But I was sick in bed at the time. It was a comforting thought that in my newfound peace, I could be with her at the spiritual level. She remains there. Her best girlfriend, an aunt, and one of my brothers were around at the time of her passing.

Recently I had a conversation with my mother's girlfriend. She agreed with me that my mom was a person of few words, and shared that she was surprised when, close to her passing, my mother enthusiastically told her that my father visited her, announcing to her that they soon would be reunited. My heart shed tears of wonderment and joy. The ways of Spirit!

✽✽✽✽✽✽✽✽

We were staying at the home of very close friends, a married couple, and a most helpful situation unfolded. The four of us were seated around a table discussing a conflict they were having around an upcoming trip. At some point in the conversation, I offered my viewpoint saying, "How about only one of you go and the other stays home?" Well this was about the worst thing I could have said as my words irritated the hell out of our woman friend, and she verbally exploded calling me "bitch" and "cunt." This was so uncharacteristic for her gentle soul. She then proceeded to say, "I want you to leave my home." This was surprising, coming as it did from a person closest to my heart. This was one of those more real than real experiences. Of course, we immediately left. The next morning, she and her husband called us and asked us to please return. We did. She apologized, and my heart accepted her apology. My husband and her husband were totally supportive, just observing the situation and mostly staying out of it. They are such old souls!

I was surprised that my reaction was not to react. In my newly found nature and inner peace I, me, simply wasn't there. The eyes of my soul were focused on the situation's emotional content, and I understood her outburst as an explosion of stuck energy that happened in a safe place. I understood that her attack was not on me, but a reflection of whatever she was dealing with, and that my job was to let that energy flow with no resistance. I simply walked away. This situation, rather than being painful and dramatic, became an opportunity for me to exercise being free of one of the burdens of being "overidentified with my identity" and, therefore, prone to defend it. Here I had the opportunity to practice being a vessel not to accumulate emotional debris, but to allow the manifested negative energy to freely pass. Following my heart, a feeling of compassion gave way to a feeling of LOVE.

I realized that Spirit had been gentle with me. This situation could have meant the end of a long and meaningful relationship. I was grateful that, even though we couldn't clearly verbalize it, we all understood how much we meant to one another.

Third Revelation

Everything returned to normal. The next day I was going about the business of the day and not thinking about anything, when suddenly I heard an inner voice saying to me:

"Love is the residual of the process of the One."

I immediately recognized the divine nature of this experience; the rational voice in me could have never come up with something so much to the point. The clarity, precision, and language indicated to me that it was a divine message.

At the personal level, I thought this message reflected on the work I had been doing addressing the nature of identity and ending with the recent event I experienced with my friend. I clearly saw that in the statement "Love is the residual of the process of the One," that love is the residual emotion of the process of letting go of the over-identification with the concept of identity. Along with this realization, there was a sense of completion and freedom in becoming more the instrument through which emotions pass and consciousness expands.

In a larger sense, I understood a bit more about energy and my role as its instrument. In the situation with my friend, the eyes of my soul saw energy releasing from my friend's energy field as my energy field moved out of the way. The emotional space where before fear would have manifested as hurt and anger, was filled with compassion that led to LOVE. I also learned that the most important lessons come from those who offer the most challenging attitudes and behavior.

Through this experience, I embodied a knowing and understanding that the concept of duality is nothing more than a construct of the mind, a habitual, ancient concept based on the perceptions of the senses of the linear world.

Afterwards, in Spirit's fashion and out of nowhere, an essential resource to apply in my spiritual unfolding showed up. In a deep meditative state of being, the letter "e" and the word "motion" dropped into my consciousness to form the word emotion. "E" meant energy and "Motion," movement. The emotions that we experience are *energy in movement*. I understood this very well and I had seen it in action.

Not too long thereafter, a second insight fell into my consciousness. It was a revision of the meaning of the word responsibility. It wasn't about the individual responsibility toward others or about the responsibility of governments toward its citizens. There was something bigger about this word. This time the word "responsibility" broke down in my mind and the eyes of my soul into two words, "response" and "ability." Suddenly this word became an active rather than a passive word, a proactive life-giving noun that, like evolution, beckons to activate more of the "abilities" to "respond" to the eternal unfolding of external and internal circumstances over which we have no control. I remembered my first shamanic experience, and this definition felt right.

Clearly, the eyes of my soul saw that as an instrument of Spirit, my main *responsibility* is to allow the unstoppable springing of emotions that life's experiences provoke to freely flow back into the life force from which they emanate. (In the perfect and divine working of the Universe, atoms and cells always self-organize, and so do we on the physical, emotional, mental, and spiritual levels.) The attachment to outcomes goes away, and that which we can't control, goes to the wayside, gradually diminishing until it disappears. The experience of life becomes more grounded and yet gentler and sacred. Simultaneously, we are able to remember and revisit our ancestors' stories without guilt, blame or shame.

The recent surprising experience with my friend was a case in point. To the degree that I was able to be fully present and grounded in my being, I was able to not respond as a victim to her words. Their negative charge didn't affect me. "Wow," I said. "This is big." I became aware that I was capable of activating new abilities to respond to a difficult situation. I had a new perspective with a focus on seeing emotions as an expression of energy. And, in doing so, I just backed away. There was no fear and no need to defend myself or my position. There was no judgment of my friend's behavior.

TEN

Divinity

As the perspectives of my soul were challenging those of my mind, another piece of insightful information came my way. In the Amazon, I heard a prophecy that speaks of a time when human societies split into two—the path of the eagle, which represents the mind, rational thought and the masculine; and the path of the condor, which represents the heart, the intuitive, and the feminine.

The prophecy tells of the time when the arrival of Cristóbal Colón (Christopher Columbus) began a period of conquest in the Americas during which the Eagle people would become so powerful that they would virtually drive the indigenous Condor people out of existence through their killing and oppression. This continues somewhat today.

The prophecy says that beginning in the 1990s, the potential would arise for these two paths to unite, and that their encounter would create a new level of human consciousness. Hmmm, this interested me deeply. I had been grappling with letting go of the world of doing where the mind's habits reign, to embrace the world of being where the heart is king. The narrative felt personal.

Mystically, my experience was illuminated by the eagle as one of my animal spirits. And my heart rejoices every time the eyes of my soul sees an eagle—including in my own neighborhood—in their great recovery from almost becoming extinct. I wondered about the condor and whether I would ever see one. I hadn't encountered any, not even when I lived in South America. But on a recent trip to Ecuador, I visited the Condor Park outside of Otavalo where there are birds of prey rescued from captivity or have been injured and cannot be returned to the wild. There, I encountered a bald eagle as I have many times before. Then as I was coming upon a pair of condors in a large enclosure, one of them suddenly took off and landed right in front of me as if it was greeting me. In this visit to the park, the mystical and physical encounter of the condor and the eagle was realized right before my eyes!

Yet, maybe because I had lived extensively both in the South and the North, the eyes of my soul saw that nothing is black and white only. Both properties and qualities of the mind and heart are essential to have a balanced life experience. My experience says though that the heart informs the mind, and that believing and acting oppositely is what causes human dysfunction.

✽✽✽✽✽✽✽✽

Off we went traveling again, this time stopping in Boulder, Colorado, to visit one of my classmates from the shamanic study program. Following her suggestion, we went to Crestone, a small spiritually focused community in the southern Colorado mountains. While there, we happened to pick up a local magazine. An advertisement of a real estate business drew my attention. In it I spotted the familiar face of a classmate from the integral incubator I participated in five years earlier. I called her, and she took us on a tour of this town near the Great Sand Dunes National Park. After we left, I got a phone call from her telling me about an upcoming integral conference based on Wilber's work. After she did a lot of negotiating to get us in at a reasonable fee, several weeks later we both met in Boulder to attend the conference.

Throughout the conference, contrary to my first experience with Wilber's theory that I thought dealt more with the masculine, there was a lot of talk about the arising of the feminine in the business world. People were talking about humanizing the workplace and seeing the workers as a source of inspiration in a co-creative process.

There was talk about waking up to the realization that we are not separate and that the world is evolving its worldview to one of evolving our innermost divine selves to serve human evolution. There was mention of outrageous love. My heart swelled with joy!

I was puzzled, though, that a couple of times when I, like other participants, wanted to voice our opinions, the facilitator—who at some point made eye contact with me hinting I would be next—ended up overlooking me. Once again, it was as if in those moments, I became invisible to him.

This experience became more real than real when toward the end of the conference, I attended a special session with Ken Wilber. Some attendees were asking about practical steps in the manifestation of the feminine. As in the conference, I raised my hand to share my opinion. But here again I remained invisible to the moderator—this time a different person. I wasn't inclined to dismiss his actions as he had played a key role throughout the conference as a master of ceremonies and had vehemently declared the value of the feminine and the surfacing of outrageous love as a Spirit's call to humanity. "What's happening," I asked myself. "Why am I being ignored?" I decided to stand up to voice my viewpoint, and he proceeded to rudely cut me off. I was not dreaming this incident. He was so rude that afterwards others in the audience came over to ask me if I was alright.

In my new understanding of responsibility, I felt fully present in the moment. I understood that I brought myself to this experience, and there was something I could learn from it. I wasn't annoyed by what had unfolded, though I wanted to figure out what was going on. Given the nature of the conference and all that was said, I considered our interaction as something of value. So, at the end of the event, I approached the man, asking him, "I am curious why you cut me off?" He immediately and emphatically responded, "Well you have to understand that there are rules. And there is a right time and place for everything. You have to be patient." To which I responded, "And who is to decide when it's the right time for the feminine to show up?" His eyes widened, and he went down on his knees saying, "Oh, my God!" I couldn't believe my eyes! I was dumbfounded! People were leaving, and that was the end of that. This all happened in seconds.

While waiting for my friends to pick me up at the hotel's lobby, this same man came by and said to me, "Hello beautiful. You are awesome!" This didn't help my understanding. At the very least, it was weird. Kind of funny, yes, but above all to my mind, sacred. Why? Because what is expressed through our words and actions is energy wanting to get through, whether we like what has happened or not in the interaction.

The magic of the circumstances was flowing, and much more happened. I met a woman, someone new to me, at one of the conference's lunches. I accepted her invitation to stay at her home on the outskirts of town. She picked me up after I attended the session I referred to, and she said to me, "You have gone through a lot. You need to rest. I will take care of you." It was uncanny for me to hear that she knew a lot had happened to me since she wasn't there with me. How did she know, I wondered?

Throughout our conversation that evening, my host kept calling me Luna. When I asked why, she just said, "That is all I see. Your name is Luna." Luna in Spanish means Moon, and my heart warmed up, feeling the deep affinity I feel with the Moon's reflecting and illuminating effect.

We went to bed, and sometime later, I got up. Entering the bathroom, I saw through its window the Orion constellation starkly clear and all by itself. I was enthralled with this vision as I had learned that in its belt there is a vast star-forming cloud. In my mind I saw the name of the constellation the way I heard it, "Ryan."

That next day I made a phone call to arrange a massage. Later on, I received a phone message showing a name I didn't recognize. I called back, and the same woman with whom I arranged the massage answered. She said she didn't call me, and she didn't recognize the name I saw on my phone's screen. When I went for the massage, I showed her the name, and we both were baffled. The name read "Gort Mhaoilir Ryan." Something popped in my brain, and seeing the word "Ryan," instantly made me remember the constellation I saw during the night. I then realized that it is called "Orion." But I was puzzled by how the name on the phone made me realize my mistake. Quite a coincidence or synchronicity? I couldn't help but wonder, as many have throughout time, if there weren't other expressions of the life force that, in this case, were communicating.

My intuitive, that is, feminine experiences with nature and Mother Earth, indicate to me that there is a lot more about life than what the rational or masculine can contemplate and understand.

Finishing this story, a few months ago I got goose bumps when I heard the words "Gort! Klaatu barada nitkol"—the most famous command in science fiction said in the movie, *The Day the Earth Stood Still*. I heard gort, the same word as on my phone, and identified him as the preserver of peace, and I thought back on Orion, the place where stars are born.

I left the conference feeling exhilarated. Life is multidimensional. My world was disintegrating and integrating all at the same time. In addition to the realization of the existence of a non-dual world, the theme of the unity of the feminine and masculine was unfolding rapidly before my eyes. I wanted to know more! Intuition and reason, the feminine and the masculine, were not just crisscrossing, but melting together. I had the insight that referring to the feminine doesn't only pertain to women. Not at all. The feminine and the masculine applies to both sexes equally and to all that exists in nature.

****

In Death Valley National Park with its salt flats, sand dunes, badlands, valleys, canyons, and mountains, I was reminded of the mystical experience where I was one with water, air, fire, and earth when they collided and life emerged. At the exhibits in the visitor's center, I was humbled to learn that the oldest rocks were formed by heat, pressure, and water that compacted at least 1.7 billion years ago. In their nature those seemingly lifeless rocks contain the memory of the history of human life and the history of all forms of life on our planet.

There, in the hottest, driest, and lowest of the national parks in the United States and standing in what is the second-lowest spot in the Western Hemisphere at 282 feet (86 meters) below sea level, I felt primordially grounded in the eternal life-giving energy. There I realized that National Parks are where the soul of the United States resides!

In the North Cascades National Park in northern Washington State, after we chatted with a park ranger for some time, she shared the location of her favorite spot in the area. We hiked to this remote place, and I couldn't resist jumping into the glacier-fed creek that vigorously rushed down from the mountains. I can never really resist jumping into rushing water. I came out of the water hearing many people talking right next to me, although no one was there. I couldn't quite make out the words they were saying. All I knew is that there was a large group of people speaking in languages unknown to me. This episode lasted several hours, and both my husband and I were perplexed. It was like the life energy of the creek and that of my body were experiencing the flow of eternal time.

The next morning, we saw the park ranger again, and I told her about my experience. Her eyes shone. She knew exactly what I was talking about, and shared that many years ago, there was a longhouse in that part of the creek where many Native American people lived, and that their Spirits are very much alive there.

Normally skinny-dipping is my favorite swimming style. But we were headed to a public hot spring in Washington on the

Olympic Peninsula. Having forgotten to bring a swimming suit, we stopped in a town to buy one. As I was trying it on, my crystal heart that I found in Brazil years before came off my necklace, hitting the floor and breaking into pieces. I felt as if my heart was breaking, too. I was in shock and surprised at my reaction. I didn't realize it at the time, but I had been working on the content of my heart and wearing a crystal heart signified my commitment. I felt heartbroken.

A few minutes later at our next stop, feeling shaky, I chose to stay in the car while my husband ran some errands. As I sat there, I closed my eyes to rest, and I began hearing Native American drumming and singing. I opened my eyes and looked out of the car's window. There was nobody around in the parking lot. I closed my eyes again and the music continued. In my mind's eye, I saw an outer circle of men drumming and singing and an inner circle made up of women dancing. I was in the center, and they were healing me. When my husband came back, I opened my eyes, and I felt renewed and joyful.

✳ ✳ ✳ ✳ ✳ ✳ ✳ ✳ ✳

Visiting the Hoh Rainforest in the Olympic National Park for the second time, we saw the devastating effects of a drought. Where three years earlier we had seen it as lush and green, it was now dry and seemingly dying. The west coast had been in a drought for a couple of years, and the rain forest was completely dried out. What a shock to see it like this. It was here we got our first experiential lessons on climate change.

A ranger told us that the snowpack on the mountains was only six percent of normal the past winter. She told us that the rangers think that humanity is in its final exam, and that the tipping point has been reached. She said that Mother Earth (Gaia) as we know it is dying, but that it will keep evolving, of course, with no regard for us as a species. The best we could hope for was the strength to cope and survive as best we could. I heard this echoed many times on our trip. Later on, in the summer, the rain forest next to the Hoh, the Quinault Rain Forest, caught on fire. Unprecedented! And the park was closed for a day (the first time in history), when hurricane force winds hit. The words "Mother Earth is dying" kept dropping their weight on my heart, and it ached when the park rangers elsewhere told us about the rapidity of glacial recession.

We continued our trip, and while in British Columbia, the reality of the deplorable state of the Earth's ecosystem became crystal clear to the eyes of my soul when I read a posted sign:

> **Please help us protect West Vancouver. This summer is like no other. Dry weather, water shortages and extreme fire risks are a real danger to our community, and require us all to think and act differently.**

I zeroed in on the words "to think and act differently." I said to myself, "Wait a minute. This sounds really familiar." An aha moment flashed within me, realizing that "to think and act differently" had also been the intent in my education work. I realized that even though the words in the public notice were spoken with regard to the human relationship with nature, it also directly applied to my personal experience when I tried to facilitate a change in attitudes and behaviors in terms of human relations in the formal education process.

I felt that something quite powerful was happening in the meeting of the ranger's words with the words on the sign. As when the children spoke their heart, the words of the rangers and the ones expressed in the public notice evoked in me a sense of urgency. I heard Spirit talking to me and to all of humanity, and it had to do with the re-balancing of the self and the elements in nature of which we humans are a byproduct.

I had mixed feelings. I was sad about the state of the environment, but happy to be aligned with the Universe! As in the past, when I heard President Obama calling "for a change of the heart of stone for a heart of flesh," which also was the intent behind my work in education, I had similar feelings.

While reflecting on these many thoughts, a light bulb turned on in my consciousness. I saw the ancient woman in my first visionary dream as Gaia, Mother Earth. She was angry at us!

****

Fourth Revelation

We returned through Chicago, and while there, like when I received the second spiritual message, this revelation came in a dream. It went like this:

A good number of people and I were at a gathering in a home. The people surrounded me and it felt like they were demanding something from me. I didn't know what it was, but I felt somewhat intimidated. I didn't know why, but I decided that my turquoise necklace would help me. I remembered I kept it in the basement. I walked down the stairs to get it.

As I begin to go down the stairs, the space felt ominous and very dark. But I found my way through it. I saw the shape of a man moving in my direction. It looked like he was going to attack me. And right before my eyes, this figure shape-shifted into a ferocious wolf. I knew I was in for the fight of my life as it tried to bite me. As I held the turquoise necklace in one hand, I was desperately groping for something to defend myself. I found a sharp knife next to me and I grabbed it, and just as the wolf was about to overcome me, I stabbed the knife into its neck. I couldn't believe I was doing this as I heard the sound of the knife brutally breaking the wolf's neck bones. But I felt all at once hopeful in the experience, though speechless and paralyzed. The wolf died, and I turned my attention to the necklace. Astoundingly, my eyes saw a scroll unfolding in slow motion out of the center of the turquoise stone. It read:

"The time has come for everyone TO BE Divine!"

with the capital letters as it reads here.

I was exhausted and rested on the shore of a large body of water. In the distance there was a jaguar swimming towards me. I felt afraid, but I had no energy to move. The jaguar came to me, caressed my face, and laid its head down on my lap like a little cat. I was astounded.

Wow, it was crystal clear to me that the emphasis on the "TO BE" was Spirit's reminder that the time has come in our evolutionary unfolding to know and understand that we are a part of the mystery of life and that we are divine.

I knew and understood that Spirit's call to humanity is to get busy doing the *being*. But I didn't know what I was to do with this information. There was no happenstance here. I took a deep breath and realized that the information relating to humanity that was locked in the turquoise stone in my necklace had been decoded!

****

Meanwhile, ever since we came back from living in Brazil, John and I were busy enjoying our time together and realizing the dream we had to travel around the country visiting national parks. But as we did, we also kept researching for places to live as we felt we had lived long enough in North Carolina and that it was time to find a new "home." Nothing materialized.

The idea of collecting ancestral memory had also caught our interest, and we decided to explore our blood ancestry via **23andMe** and later on through **ancestry.com.** We were excited about the reports. There was such precision in the DNA information that John received. It included, for example, the name of the little town in County Mayo, Ireland, where his father's mother came from and the region in Sweden from where his mother's parents had emigrated.

In my case, I knew that like most Colombian people, I was a "mestiza," meaning a mix of Native and European ancestry. I was quite surprised though when my results indicated that I have forty-four percent Native American blood. This was empowering as it reaffirmed my gut reaction, my blood boiling inside me, when I perceived the pervasive mistreatment of others toward Native American people!

Interestingly, many years earlier, when I was not aware that the human experience had a lot to do with collecting ancestral memories, John and I visited China. It was heartwarming to find peoples' features and spirits familiar. Recently I saw a timeline map of the 200,000-year-history of human civilization on **kottke.org.** There I was reminded about the migration of the very earliest people from Asia to the Americas and to South America, in particular.

Related to the larger picture about humanity that interested my soul so deeply, I felt further empowered seeing that this kind of scientific information technology is symbolic of the coming together of the heart/intuition/feminine and the mind/reason/masculine. This is very much like the prophecy of the condor and the eagle. This was a reaffirmation about trusting the wisdom of my ancestors!

Wanting to further explore my ancestry, we made plans to go to Spain. Prior to our trip, I went to see a medicine person asking Spirit to tell me about where "home" was for us. The medicine person told me that I needed to go to no other place but Spain, specifically southern Spain! That home was there. This was exciting news, and my mind quickly envisioned an actual place there. But, how did she know we were going to Spain? Ah, the way of Spirit. The plot was thickening.

One night, shortly before we were leaving for our first visit to Spain, I was sharing with girlfriends about my long and difficult spiritual journey since closing my agency and I told them I had become a hermit. One of them, no doubt an angel, mentioned the book *La Noche Oscura*, (*The Dark Night*). The next day I downloaded the book onto my computer. It was written by San Juan de la Cruz (Saint John of the Cross), a sixteenth century Spanish mystic, and I read it as though its message was directed at me. There was no doubt after reading it that I had lived through a dark night.

I was really interested in how San Juan divides the passage of *The Dark Night* into the dark night of the senses and voluntary self-discipline, and the dark night of the spirit. In the former, he says one works with the physical, and in the latter, Spirit works on the soul. It profoundly resonated within me. I was ready to know more!

Excitedly, I told John about what I had read, and we decided to visit as many places as possible related to San Juan, following the Saint's path in Southern Spain, which mystically happens to be the same region my DNA study says my ancestry comes from. Well, for all practical purposes, this trip became our first spiritual pilgrimage.

Of the many sites we visited, we encountered a lovely monastery on the outskirts of Segovia where the saint lived for a while. We were given the keys to his small chapel on the top of a hill above the monastery where the Saint went to pray daily. There we experienced a heavy, thunderous storm and the appearance of a rainbow, all within minutes. We went back to the monastery where we had a lovely visit with the abbot, Salvador Ros Garcia. He took us to a cave below the monastery where the mystic once lived. Wow! This was some reality of collecting memories!

Afterwards, he invited us to participate in a service offered in the chapel, and I was both surprised and honored when I was asked to read the Epistle. All these experiences were quite special.

Then the abbot and I sat around the central court of this ancient monastery, the sun shining upon us. In the shadow of the history, memories, and mysteries of the place, I shared with him about my revelations and my desire to put it all together in a book. He encouraged me to do so.

I bought the abbot's book *La Experiencia de Dios en Mitad de la Vida* (*The Experience of God at Midlife*), which is a commentary about the *Dark Night*, and another book, *Silent Music—The Life, Work, and Thought of St. John of the Cross* by R. A. Herrera. Ros Garcia signed his book and wrote the following "To Aura, with a wish that this book helps her to see (to see is to understand) her multiple experiences of God."

We walked the saint's path through the ancient hills back to our hotel in the center of Segovia's old town in the colonnade of the Plaza Mayor. All that had transpired had been a most humbling experience. The monastery, the Saint's cave, and his personal chapel on the hill—they all felt like sacred temples.

We had a quiet dinner and then went to our room. From our room's balcony at almost arm's reach was the Church of San Miguel where Isabella was proclaimed Queen of Castile in 1474. I contemplated the passing of time and history. Never in my imagination did I dream to be in such a consequential place in the world of doing.

I woke up the next morning hearing in my mind in my half-awake state "Tienes que escribir en Español!" "You must write in Spanish!" A rush of energy went through my being, and I felt exhilarated. It became evident that writing in my native tongue was the means for me to give credit to the heavy weight of the memories of emotional pain my heart had been carrying since my childhood. After all, the memories were stored in my mind in Spanish. For the first time in my life, I became emotionally naked to myself, looking at fear straight in the eye.

The simplicity and directness of the message was what I'd learned to recognize and trust as Spirit's insight for me. At this point in my journey, there was no doubting or questioning Spirit's instruction.

Healing of the Heart
When I got back home, I began writing in Spanish and a painful, fierce, and sorrowful process followed. It consumed my existence as a torrent of memories and emotions of a man-made world of suffering and pain, like the waves of a roaring sea, surfaced. Tears flooded my whole being. I cried and wrote, and then I cried about what I wrote. Days, hours, minutes, and seconds passed, while in body, mind, and spirit, I contemplated, acknowledged, and honored the pain, anger, sadness, and shame that memories of my childhood, adolescence, and young adulthood evoked. Somehow, I knew I was not only crying my own tears, but those of my parents and other ancestors from the beginning of life on Earth.

The more I wrote, long and forgotten memories about my parents' lives took a front row, and my heart opened to acknowledge and honor their story. Memories of things I knew, but had long forgotten about their lives revisited me. Throughout, it was clear that I was not seeking justification for my parents' hurtful behavior and attitudes. It was all about understanding what caused them in the first place. In this understanding I found a sense of compassion for them and for me and others in my family.

I mentioned previously that my father, from the time he was fourteen, became the sole supporter of his mother, my grandmother. Now I wondered about her own childhood and her ancestral memories that made her be a withdrawn and somewhat cold person.

My mother was the only child of her mother's first marriage. She lost her father in a car accident when she was a young child. When my grandmother remarried, my mother's life became miserable because her new step siblings treated her like an outsider. She escaped a hostile family environment, marrying my father who she met at work. She was fourteen and he was seventeen. Their life together was a struggle from the beginning, trying to make sense of a life without a childhood and without love. In my experience of them, they never could come to acknowledge or much less, honor that. This explained my feeling as a child that there was something wrong in their life, something I really couldn't understand.

My mother was the only person who showed interest in my formal education. Whether aware of it or not, she always sought to provide me and my brothers with something she couldn't have. She made sure I attended school, and she managed to somehow expose me to a variety of extracurricular activities— a classical ballet program, being a contestant on a dance program on national television along with one of my brothers, and participating in a couple of beauty contests when I was six and sixteen years old. My mother's tenacity, resourcefulness, and effectiveness in her younger years were something I know I inherited from her. I came to understand that all she did for me were acts of love.

Her submissiveness to my father pushed me to find the courage to always be myself despite anything. My father's rudeness pushed me to maintain my decency no matter what. I hated what I perceived to be my father's scarcity syndrome and my mother's submissiveness to his extreme authoritarian ways. I felt frustrated that I couldn't change any of this.

Now I understood that whatever their spiritual contract was, they were handicapped living together in a relationship that appeared sometimes fragile and sometimes strong. I acquired compassion toward their individual attempted suicides, and my heart warmed up remembering that they grew closer as they became elderly.

Increasingly, amongst emotions and tears, I became aware that my parents did the best they could. I was grateful that the hands of Spirit—my intuition—guided me to not use drugs, get pregnant, or marry to escape my family's toxicity. I was grateful that I made the choice to leave home only when I felt ready to organize my own life. And I was grateful that I, against all odds, was graced in finding a soul mate with similar values and an enduring and loving relationship.

Spirit illuminated my experience with the opportunity to practice the kind of response + ability that is based on not letting limitations of the past influence what feels right in the present moment. It felt good to realize that I hadn't internalized behaviors and attitudes from them that intuitively didn't feel right. It had evoked in me a sense of integrity.

Being with my parents was not easy, and yet it was to be the basis for so much of my learning. The ways in which my parents failed me and my brothers were a result of the limiting beliefs, self-sabotaging behaviors, and negative patterns they acquired as children as they learned to do whatever they felt it took to survive.

In the spiritual sense, my father and mother were my great teachers. I learned that they sacrificed their lives in the linear world to provide for experiences to challenge my spiritual evolution. This is a highest expression of love.

During this time of reflection about their lives where there had been pain and an emotional distance in my heart, I, for the first time, felt gratitude toward my parents and myself. Ah, the ways of Spirit!

Recently John and I went to the birthday party of Nicoyembe, an old friend in Colombia. He is a national figure in the world of African folklore music, and his party was a well-deserved grand celebration with the participation of a great variety of musical groups representing the country's cultures. As the party went on and I danced and danced, I entered into a spiritual space. The occasion became a religious experience to honor my parents' lives.

✽✽✽✽✽✽✽✽

Throughout my journey I learned that the human experience is informed by primal and ancestral memories and the memories we make throughout our own lives. Collecting primal and ancestral memories, I experienced the full spectrum of powerful emotions, from unspeakable pain to celestial bliss. But collecting my memories from my own personal life was a very different and difficult experience. Fear kept me from facing the content of my heart, the first revelation I received.

As I began to write in Spanish, the story of my life appeared before my eyes. No longer was there the focus my mind had maintained writing about my work in English. It was as if I was peeling off layers of an onion—I began experiencing my emotional body's wounds that were well hidden deep inside. Herein was the meaning of a dream that for several years kept on recurring. I wanted to be naked and something would stop me. I felt afraid and ashamed even when others didn't notice me.

Writing about my life, I finally crossed the emotional barrier I built as a child to survive and gave myself permission to make a big deal out of my past to recover my present. As I did, my silent shame and self-pity disappeared, and I began recovering my own humanity. The tears I cried were not only about my own memories of emotional pain, but that of my parents and other ancestors. We are, after all, connected in our fear, pain, and love.

Intuitively all my life I'd been seeking harmony. I left my parent's home without achieving it, and I carried the desire to do so into the World where it passionately manifested in my social activism. But I've learned that the soul doesn't care about what we humans do in the World. It only cares about how we evolve spiritually.

Spirit reminds us that we are instruments in the evolutionary process of consciousness that is always reflecting on the world outside. Aha, this was what spiritual guides quite a long time ago meant when they said, "Do not, for a moment, doubt the power of stillness and peace. The divine light shines through the darkest of caves."

The spiritual guides were referring to the divine power that emanates from within the inner cave when, after departing from the paradigm of living our life based solely in the perception of a linear world in the dark night of the senses, the self is silenced, and Spirit, in the stillness of the dark night of spirit, communicates eternal wisdom. Now I understood the division that San Juan de la Cruz made of the dark night.

Grappling with the content of my heart, I felt like a river that has been cleaned up and begins to freely flow and restore its ecosystem. Besides becoming lighter, my heart began to transform from stony and stubborn into a tender, responsive heart willing to freely process the emotions the human experience of life evoke and that serve the evolution of consciousness. This I realized is the function of human life. Period.

ELEVEN

Transcendence

Contemporary Mysticism

Karl Rahner, a German theologian, which many consider to be the foremost Roman Catholic thinker of the 20th century says, "...the spirituality of the future will not be based any longer in a unanimous, evident and public conviction, nor in a religious generalized environment prior to the personal experience and decision." My life story fits this description perfectly.

Personal experience and decision are the basis of all that I have shared in this book. My journey is a testament to an intuitive and conscious practice of discernment using faith, intuition, insights, and a connection with nature. These are the sacred instruments through which Spirit has guided my quest for answers. I have come to see that their truth informs my moral compass and my choices.

Something else became obvious when I read Herrera's *Silent Music*. He writes, "The mystic is not a dreamer, or a self-inflated psychopath and her point of departure is a hard-nosed appraisal of the human condition. The isolated phenomena in which spiritual accounts abound, no matter how elevated, do not make a mystical life. These phenomena must be integrated, must respond to a principle of organization, must form a structure, an organism, to be so identified."

I began to connect all the dots between these concepts and my experiences. Early in my life, I met fear face to face. Being near-blind until the age of sixteen metaphorically illustrates the somberness about the external world that preoccupied my soul as well as the bright flame of faith in the life force within that illuminated my choices. To survive fear, I developed coping defense mechanisms that kept me distant from my vulnerabilities.

As an adult I became a warrior projecting my soul's desire for harmony into the world. For a long time in my work with my non-profit agency, I felt that I was on the right path. But after two decades of struggle, something felt missing in my quest. That began to change with my first visionary dream, the first of four revelations Spirit delivered to me. It said, "All is well when the content of the heart is considered." At the time, my mind couldn't understand what this meant.

A year later, a second divine revelation asked, "How long are you willing to see things only half true and remain in darkness?" My mind, afraid of half-truths and darkness, went berserk.

Time passed, and I grew more and more uncomfortable and disillusioned with the World. Children told me that fear is what causes the human dysfunction. It rang a bell, although I still had deaf ears. My heart began to suffocate. What had happened to my sense of security and purpose? *I'd entered the dark night of the senses.*

I felt emotionally and physically paralyzed. I knew I had to decide whether to live or die. I came to make a conscious decision to live, no longer trusting only the self and reason to inform my choices. I surrendered, asking Spirit to show me the way, to tell me the truth about what was essential.

My mind began growing quieter and I, for the first time in my life, recognized that I was not in control of anything that happens in the world. Half of my perceptions about the World were evaporating, while the space that they occupied in my consciousness was being filled with spiritual content. I'd experienced the highs and lows of the dark night of the senses. And my mind was illuminated with the understanding of oneness and nonduality. I experienced love as the creative energy in motion that unifies my experience of the life process.

Ten years passed, and Spirit communicated another divine revelation, "Love is the residual of the process of the one." I understood what that meant because of my previous insights on oneness and nonduality.

A year later, Spirit communicated a final revelation, "The time has come for everyone To Be Divine." This is a wakeup call to humanity to transcend the paradigm of living solely "to do" into a paradigm of living solely "to be" within the understanding that we are an integral part of divinity.

The four divine revelations were interconnected, organized, structured, and centered around the healing of my heart and connected me to the divine and sacred. The time in between them was spent in the process of bringing my mind and heart together.

But the conclusiveness and clarity of these last revelations didn't come across in my writing. I kept asking Spirit what was missing, and this is when I read *The Dark Night*. Shortly afterwards John and I made a trip to Segovia in southern Spain to where he lived, and I heard the command to write in my native language, Spanish.

Spirit showed me a four-step process for the advancement of human consciousness. It connects the human experience to the divine which, intuitively, had been the focus of my soul's attention since childhood. My life was consumed by full-blown mystical experiences. No doubt, I've lived the life of a contemporary mystic.

Mother Nature

Throughout my journey, many times I asked myself, "where is the soul in the physical world around me?" I couldn't feel it in the neighborhoods, the schools, or in the shopping centers. As a child, I certainly didn't see it in my parents. I couldn't see where God was. Something was missing. Where was the soul?

Well, one day, while visiting Death Valley National Park, boom! The eyes of my soul spotted something important. I realized that the soul resides in the national parks, in raw nature! How could it not be thus? Nature *is* the soul of Mother Earth. And we humans don't just live in nature. We are nature.

The books say that nature is the natural, physical, or material world or universe. They say that humans are considered part of nature, but human activity is often understood as a separate category from other natural phenomena. This contradicted my experience. Everything in the universe including human activity is natural phenomena. All that "is" is intrinsically interconnected. Period.

I intuitively knew this as a child. Memories visited me again of my loneliness when nature evoked in me peace and a sense of sufficiency in an otherwise deficient human world. There, in its silence, I heard the movement of energy in the water, the air, the flowers, the birds, and the clouds. They communicated something ethereal and eternal. The army of ants that went through our house at my parents' farm also came to mind. I saw a direct connection between their rigorous disciplined effort and that of the most disciplined human army. Clearly, whether instinctual or rational, each is an expression of the life force and consciousness in action that is always in the driver's seat.

When I was a bit older, in nature I felt resonance with the content of my soul and the harmony I sought as a child. In nature I felt the power of intuition and insight fully manifested connecting mind and heart. As an adult, assisted by the medicinal plant San Pedro, I viscerally participated in the life-making process and felt the interconnectedness of all that is. I encountered the pure essence of being. It was also in nature, in its temple in the Amazon, where I found that what my mind had characterized as ethereal and eternal was God residing within me.

I found the great disconnect that negatively affects the human experience. A disconnect from nature gives power to recurring thought forms and conditioned mental and emotional patterns that are invested in the overidentification of the sense of the "I," the ego, in the world of doing. In this world, overblown egos in positions of power and leadership seek to self-preserve and deliver, manipulate, and perpetuate social constructs like race, religion, politics, social class, gender identity, and sexual preference. Overblown egos in positions of victimhood do their part by thriving on the constant blame, finger-pointing, and self-pity that are fueled by pessimism and anger. It's a vicious circle.

Whether it happens in a conscious or unconscious manner, the result is the same, and the preservation of the wants and desires of overblown egos is what nurtures the culture of fear of one another that still prevails today.

> "What is needed now, more than ever, is leadership that steers us away from fear and fosters greater confidence in the inherent goodness and ingenuity of humanity."
> —The Honorable Jimmy Carter

The Power of Faith, Intuition, Insight, and Choice

We often recognize intuition only in hindsight. It is when something feels right and moves us to act. Insight is when something feels lifegiving and is powerful enough to obliterate long-held beliefs and habits, and we are moved to think and act differently. I knew about this experientially when I distanced myself from some of my parents' attitudes and behaviors, and from, among other experiences like my flight from the bullfight, stopping the consumption of sugar, and entering my dark night.

Passing through the dark night of the senses, Spirit forced me to face losing my attachment to the false sense of invulnerability I'd relied upon all my life. I had to let go of the ways of the warrior I became to survive in a world that didn't recognize my pain or my soul's desire for harmony. I experienced what I believe to be the greatest fear in the human experience, the death of the self. How strange to be afraid of something that doesn't really exist!

In my experience, what died was the paradigm of living my life with a focus only on the mind-based, physical, linear, rational, and masculine world to make sense of my existence.

Embracing change, I entered the dark night of spirit and began the paradigm of living my life with a focus on the heart-based, intuitive, spiritual, and feminine world.

My heart and mind came together to identify and nurture the spiritual and rational qualities that best express one's divine essence in the world. This was the final message from Spirit, "The time has come for everyone To Be Divine."

Uprooting Fear
No matter where it comes from or what it is about, facing fear taught me that I am neither my mind, nor my memories. I am consciousness. Nevertheless, I discovered that by acknowledging and honoring the emotions that fear evoked in my body and mind directly affected my well-being, especially, the fluidity of my heart.

Nevertheless, managing fear still continues to be a work in progress, particularly when confronting the past. Not too long ago, I was driving home when suddenly I felt a terrible apprehension and anxiety. My heart began beating rapidly—my hands were sweaty. I had to stop the car. "What's going on?" I asked myself. I was close to having a panic attack. I checked inside myself, and I knew I had nothing to worry about. I realized that I was regressing to a time when I was afraid of going home because I never knew what awful news was awaiting me or afraid my father would find a reason to beat me again.

Memories are energy, as are words, and emotions are energy in motion as previous insights indicated to me. When memories of fear or any of its derivatives get stuck, there is pain that blocks the heart and blurs the mind. Emotions always begin flowing freely when attachment to that memory goes by the wayside.

I learned that only by recovering the fluidity of the heart can we adequately process the unstoppable springing of emotions that life's experiences provoke, allowing them to freely flow back into the life force from which they sprang. Herein, finally, was the realization of the first divine message I received, "All is well when the content of the heart is considered."

****

On my journey I learned that spiritually there is nothing intrinsically right or wrong, not good or bad. In every human being, deep down, is a knowing about what is life giving or what is not—as well as the free will to choose between the two. I learned that to live in the harmony we seek, we must activate our capacity to be, to act out our divinity. This defines our individual and collective life experiences, which reflect in the state of the world.

My experience informs us that today we are entrenched in a collective dark night of the senses, and that the time has come for us to move into the collective dark night of the Spirit. To do so, we must build the courage to choose and use the tools of Spirit—our faith, intuition, and insights.

We must overcome the prejudice against "trusting our gut feeling" or "following our heart." Even though we hear these expressions a lot, they are often put down as "woo-woo" stuff—unworthy of serious consideration. At the heart of this ambivalence are the cracks we perceive in the world we create. But they are visionary and prescient—attributes of the intuitive.

My father was an example of the contradiction that humanity is facing between the fear manifested in the authoritarianism, distrust, and belligerence that pervades our World and the love embedded in our hearts. A story my nephew shared with me some time ago brought this contradiction to mind. One day my father tearfully showed him a little bird he was trying to save from dying. This was so out of character. My nephew went on to study psychology trying to understand this disconnect between the intuitive love that moved my father to compassion and the irrational fear that pervaded his life that manifested in his violent machismo.

We must address the dissonance between our soul's desire, which is expressed intuitively and through insight, and our mind's needs and wants, which are expressed rationally in patterns of thought and conditioned attitudes and behaviors. No amount of "doing" by the habitual self as humanist, social activist, entrepreneur, financier, politician, priest, shaman, or whomever else can resolve the dissonance between our mind and our soul.

Only by fully embracing, acknowledging, and honoring the dark night of the senses and of spirit and addressing the content of our heart will we see the face of God and our divinity. And only by embracing, acknowledging, and honoring Mother Nature will we find our intuition and insights heightening and informing the moral compass that we desperately and instinctively seek. Only then will we find spiritual, mental, emotional, and physical integrity to be and consciously act, not just do.

In the twenty-first century each one of us has the moral responsibility to face fear right in the eye and use the conundrum of living in the age of information and knowledge that confuses the mind, to practice the life-giving power of discernment to define our moral compass and our choices. We all possess the faith, intuition, and insight to do so. We all have the spiritual tools and instruments to overcome the night of the senses and arrive at the night of spirit to see not fear, but our own divinity.

A Navajo Story
An old man and his grandson went walking in the woods. The Navajo spoke to his grandson, teaching him about the plants to eat and the plants to avoid, and teaching him how to read the story written in the dusty earth by the paw tracks of animals. When the old man saw that two wolves had traveled across their path, he knelt at the tracks and turned to his grandson to teach him of spirit. He said to the boy, "Grandson, there are two wolves in your heart fighting for your attention."

"It's a terrible fight between two wolves. One is evil, snarling with rage. He is full of anger, envy, sorrow, regret, greed, arrogance, self-pity, guilt, resentment, inferiority, lies, false pride, superiority, and ego. The other is good, howling in harmony with the moon and all living things. He is joy, peace, love, hope, serenity, humility, kindness, benevolence, empathy, generosity, truth, compassion, and faith. As you grow up, the fight will grow stronger between these two wolves. And everyone in the human race will face this same fight!"

"Which wolf will win?" the boy asked his Grandfather. He said, "The answer is simple… The one you feed!"

All is well when the content of the Heart is considered.

www.ingramcontent.com/pod-product-compliance
Lightning Source LLC
Chambersburg PA
CBHW032358100526
44587CB00010BA/288